WRITERS AND THEIR W...

ISOBEL ARMSTRONG
Consultant Editor

PENELOPE FITZGERALD

PENELOPE FITZGERALD

Hugh Adlington

© Copyright 2018 by Hugh Adlington

First published in 2018 by
Liverpool University Press
4 Cambridge Street
Liverpool L69 7ZU

on behalf of
Northcote House Publishers Ltd
Mary Tavy
Devon PL19 9PY

All rights reserved. No part of this work may be reproduced or stored in an information retrieval system (other than short extracts for the purposes of review) without the express permission of the Publishers given in writing.

British Library Cataloguing-in-Publication Data
A catalogue record for this book is available from the British Library

ISBN 978-0-7463-1294-0 hardcover
ISBN 978-0-7463-1295-7 paperback

Typeset by PDQ Typesetting, Newcastle-under-Lyme
Printed and bound in Poland by BooksFactory.co.uk

In loving memory of Rose Frances

Contents

Acknowledgements	ix
Biographical Outline	xi
Abbreviations and References	xiii
Introduction	1
1 Critical Writing	9
2 Biographies	21
Edward Burne-Jones	22
The Knox Brothers	26
Charlotte Mew and Her Friends	32
3 Early Novels	36
The Golden Child	37
The Bookshop	42
Offshore	48
Human Voices	54
At Freddie's	60
4 Late Novels	67
Innocence	69
The Beginning of Spring	78
The Gate of Angels	87
The Blue Flower	93

5 Short Stories, Poems, Letters	101
6 Reputation and Influence	113
Appendix: Uncollected and Unattributed Poems	118
Notes	120
Select Bibliography	132
Index	143

Acknowledgements

I wish to thank above all Terence Dooley, Penelope Fitzgerald's literary executor, for his generous encouragement and invaluable comments. I also wish to give special thanks to Hermione Lee for her *Penelope Fitzgerald: A Life*, the starting point for all serious scholarship on Fitzgerald's life and writing. I am grateful to the publishers of Penelope Fitzgerald's work and of other copyright material, and to the Harry Ransom Center at Austin, University of Texas for granting me access to Penelope Fitzgerald's working papers. Everything else I owe to Kate, our son Michael, and our daughter Rose, to whose memory the book is dedicated.

Biographical Outline

1916	Born in Hampstead, London.
1930–5	Attends Wycombe Abbey School; writes for the school magazine, the *Wycombe Abbey Gazette*.
1935	Offered Senior Scholarship (for best candidate in her year) by Somerville College, University of Oxford.
1938	Graduates with congratulatory First Class degree.
1937–48	Writes reviews for *Punch*; works at the BBC.
1942	Marries Desmond Fitzgerald.
1950–3	Edits (with Desmond) *World Review*.
1956–8	Writes serial for *Swift*, called 'Jassy of Juniper Farm'.
1957–61	Lives in Southwold, Suffolk; works part-time in the Sole Bay Bookshop.
1960	Moves family back to London; lives on houseboat, *Grace*.
1960–87	Teaches at Italia Conti stage school, Queen's Gate School and Westminster Tutors.
1963	Houseboat sinks; Fitzgerald and daughters sent to London County Council Centre for the Homeless, Hackney Wick, E9.
1964	Family move to Poynders Gardens, London SW4.
1974	Her short story, 'The Axe', shortlisted for *Times* ghost-story competition; published in *The Times Anthology of Ghost Stories* (1975).
1975	*Edward Burne-Jones: A Biography* published; Desmond dies.
1977	*The Knox Brothers* published; *The Golden Child*, Fitzgerald's first novel, published.

BIOGRAPHICAL OUTLINE

1978	*The Bookshop* published; shortlisted for Booker Prize.
1979	*Offshore* published; wins Booker Prize.
1980	*Human Voices* published.
1980–2000	Writes over 200 book reviews for numerous publications.
1982	*At Freddie's* published.
1984	*Charlotte Mew and Her Friends*, Fitzgerald's third biography, published; wins British Academy Crawshay Prize (1985).
1986	*Innocence* published.
1988	*The Beginning of Spring* published; shortlisted for Booker Prize.
1990	*The Gate of Angels* published; shortlisted for Booker Prize.
1995	*The Blue Flower* published. Awarded the Heywood Hill Literary Prize for lifelong contribution to the enjoyment of books.
1998	*The Blue Flower* wins US National Book Critics' Circle Award.
2000	Dies; *The Means of Escape*, a collection of Fitzgerald's short stories, published.
2003	*A House of Air: Selected Writings* published.
2008	*So I Have Thought of You: The Letters of Penelope Fitzgerald* published.
2013	*Penelope Fitzgerald: A Life*, by Hermione Lee, published.

Abbreviations

AF	*At Freddie's* (London: Fourth Estate, 2013)
BF	*The Blue Flower* (London: Fourth Estate, 2013)
BK	*The Bookshop* (London: Fourth Estate, 2013)
BS	*The Beginning of Spring* (London: Fourth Estate, 2014)
CM	*Charlotte Mew and Her Friends: with a Selection of Her Poems* (London: Fourth Estate, 2014)
EB	*Edward Burne-Jones* (London: Fourth Estate, 2014)
GA	*The Gate of Angels* (London: Fourth Estate, 2014)
GC	*The Golden Child* (London: Fourth Estate, 2014)
HA	*A House of Air*, intro. Hermione Lee (London: Harper Perennial, 2009)
HR	*Hudson Review*
HRC	Harry Ransom Center at Austin, University of Texas
HV	*Human Voices* (London: Fourth Estate, 2014)
IN	*Innocence* (London: Fourth Estate, 2013)
KB	*The Knox Brothers* (London: Fourth Estate, 2013)
LRB	*London Review of Books*
LATBR	*Los Angeles Times Book Review*
ME	*The Means of Escape: Stories* (London: Flamingo, 2000)
NYRB	*New York Review of Books*
NYTBR	*New York Times Book Review*
OF	*Offshore* (London: Fourth Estate, 2013)
PF	*Penelope Fitzgerald: A Life*, Hermione Lee (London: Chatto & Windus, 2013)
SI	*So I Have Thought of You: The Letters of Penelope Fitzgerald*, ed., Terence Dooley (London: Fourth Estate, 2009)
TLS	*Times Literary Supplement*
WR	*World Review*

... 'the land that is more true than real'.
Penelope Fitzgerald, *Edward Burne-Jones: A Biography* (1975), 226

I kept on asking myself, 'How is it done?'
C. K. Stead, *London Review of Books* (9 Oct 1988), 22

Introduction

Penelope Fitzgerald has been acclaimed as one of the finest, if most enigmatic, British novelists of the late twentieth century. Nearly sixty when her first book was published, she went on to write nine novels, four of which were shortlisted for the Booker Prize, and one of which, *Offshore*, won. Her final work of fiction, *The Blue Flower*, won the prestigious US National Book Critics' Circle Award. She also wrote three biographies, a collection of short stories and countless critical essays and book reviews. Fitzgerald's works are distinguished by their acute wit, deft handling of emotional tone and unsentimental yet deeply felt commitment to portraying the lives of outsiders: those men, women and children 'who seem to have been born defeated or, even, profoundly lost' (*HA* 508). Miracles of compression, her slender tragicomic fictions somehow contain worlds, transporting us to post-war London, Suffolk and Florence, pre-revolutionary Russia, Edwardian Cambridge and late eighteenth-century Saxony. Her style is deceptively simple yet an inclination towards the metaphysical, oblique and absurd is never far from the seemingly unruffled surface of her prose. The resulting sensation, as Fitzgerald said of reading E. M. Forster, is like 'drinking strong wine out of a teacup – puzzling, not quite right perhaps, but in the end...all the more effective'.[1] The strangeness of this effect has often been noted, yet the means by which she achieved it remain a mystery. Invariably readers ask, 'How is it done?' This book aims to answer that question.

Fitzgerald's life provides some clues. Born in 1916, Penelope Mary Knox grew up in a family of writers: 'where everyone was publishing, or about to publish, something' (*HA* 495). Her father was the comic journalist and poet E. V. ('Evoe') Knox, editor of *Punch*; her mother, Christina, contributed to the *Manchester*

1

Guardian and Macmillan's English Literature Series of abridged classic texts; her aunt, Winifred Peck, wrote more than twenty novels; and her three uncles, Dillwyn, Wilfred and Ronald were distinguished scholars and thinkers, variously translators of ancient Greek poetry and the Latin Vulgate Bible, decipherers of enemy codes in two world wars, and writers of biblical commentary, Roman Catholic apologetics and detective novels. Wilfred and Ronald were ordained ministers – another family tradition: both of Fitzgerald's grandfathers served as Evangelical bishops in the Church of England.

From her earliest days, Fitzgerald imbibed a culture of putting words together. Rhyme sheets from the Poetry Bookshop, back numbers of *Punch*, the yarns and tales of the periodicals of the day, Walter de la Mare's *Peacock Pie* and the family magazine (*IF, or Howl Ye Bloodhounds*), all fuelled Fitzgerald's love of reading and writing. At Wycombe Abbey School, Fitzgerald (known in the family as 'Mops' or 'Mopsa', after the young shepherdess in *The Winter's Tale*) kept a commonplace book, sent home a weekly illustrated news-sheet ('Wuffine News') and was the chief contributor to the school magazine (*PF* 30–8). In 1935 Fitzgerald was offered a Senior Scholarship (for best candidate in her year) by Somerville College, Oxford, her mother's college. Her mother died suddenly that same year. During her time at Oxford Fitzgerald co-edited The *Cherwell*, the University newspaper, and wrote articles and other pieces of student journalism. She graduated with a congratulatory First Class degree in English Literature and Language in 1938, fully intending to become an author: 'I have been reading steadily for seventeen years; when I go down I want to start writing'[2] (*PF* 55–62). She was as good as her word. Between 1937 and 1948, Fitzgerald wrote more than fifty book, film and theatre reviews for *Punch* (doubtless it helped that her father was Editor).

Stylistic elements characteristic of her novels are present in even the earliest of her *Punch* reviews. In 1939, Fitzgerald reported on the international horse show at Olympia:

> All horses, they say, are fit for heaven, and Olympia brings together the fittest of all; indeed, the class of entry this year was so high that the average hippophile could forget the hardness of the seats in pure admiration and envy – emotions just as good for the soul, by the way, as pity and terror.[3]

INTRODUCTION

Disarmingly ironical in the *Punch* style, Fitzgerald's writing here includes at least two features characteristic of her fiction: the authoritative adage passed off as common knowledge ('All horses, they say, are fit for heaven'), and the unexpected swerve from received wisdom – here Fitzgerald stands up for the less exalted feelings of admiration and envy.[4] In this period she also wrote radio scripts for the BBC, chiefly for the Schools Service. She would later draw on her wartime BBC experience for her fourth novel, *Human Voices*. In 1942 she married Irish Guardsman Desmond Fitzgerald, and in the first four years of married life, in which she continued reviewing and writing scripts, she suffered at least one miscarriage and the death of a baby shortly after birth.

It is misleading, then, to present Fitzgerald as a 'late-starter' as critics often do. She wrote constantly through her first three decades, and there is little mystery as to why her first book wasn't published until she was fifty-nine years old. Childrearing, a difficult marriage to a troubled husband and the demands of teaching left little time for the kind of sustained writing it takes to complete a book. With the birth of a son, Valpy, in 1947, Fitzgerald gave up reviewing for *Punch*, and three years later Christina ('Tina') was born. Yet even with two young children Fitzgerald still threw herself for almost three years into editing, with her husband Desmond, the monthly *World Review*, 'a magazine of the Arts, Politics and Law', for which she wrote editorial articles and reviews.[5] In 1953, however, the magazine folded, her third child (Maria, or 'Ria') was born, and the years that followed were increasingly difficult. Fitzgerald may have suffered further miscarriages and there were constant financial worries. Short of money, the family moved to Southwold, Suffolk in 1957, where Fitzgerald worked part-time in a bookshop, an experience she later drew on for her novel, *The Bookshop*. Financial necessity drove the family back to London in 1961 to live on a houseboat, *Grace*, and Fitzgerald took teaching jobs at the Italia Conti stage school, Queen's Gate School and Westminster Tutors. The period on the houseboat provided the setting for *Offshore*. Teaching at stage school she turned into fiction in *At Freddie's*. When *Grace* sank into the Thames, the family were placed in sheltered accommodation before moving to a council flat in Clapham, south

London. Looking back in old age, Fitzgerald remembered her aunt, Winifred Peck, who wrote all of her life: 'I would rather have liked to have done that myself, write all my life, but that just wasn't possible in my case. I had a family to raise.'[6] Yet even though her first book came late, in 1975, Fitzgerald had in fact by then been writing, on and off, for fifty years.

Even the most difficult years in the 1960s had a part to play in Fitzgerald's development as a writer. As Hermione Lee's superb biography shows, teaching, for all its tribulations, allowed Fitzgerald to think and speak from the writer's point of view: 'she taught literature like a novelist, always bringing the text back to the stuff of experience and getting us to look at *how it was being done*' (*PF* 197). Fitzgerald's teaching notes reveal glimpses of interests familiar from her fiction. Samuel Beckett's stoicism and dialogues between mind and body fascinated her, as did questions of morality and self-deception in Jane Austen. Emotions she preferred to be kept in check; she noticed minor characters and was sympathetic towards the lives of women (*PF* 200–1). Critical touchstones for her teaching included W. J. Harvey's *Character and the Novel*, George Steiner's *Language and Silence*, and Frank Kermode's *The Sense of an Ending* (*PF* 198). All three authors shared with Fitzgerald the experience of having lived through the Second World War and the moral seriousness in relation to literature, education and language that that experience engendered. All three were committed, as Fitzgerald was in her teaching and later in her writing, to the idea of 'the complex miracle of ... great art, of what answer we can give to it from our own being'.[7] Nor was Fitzgerald's appetite for beauty, culture and language blunted by work and family duties in these years. She read ceaselessly, followed radio and television, and went as often as she could to the cinema, theatre, ballet, exhibitions and pottery classes; she learned languages and travelled widely, at home and abroad (*PF* 163–7). When the Fitzgerald's younger daughter, Maria, graduated from Oxford in 1974 and there were no longer children at home, Fitzgerald was freer to write. In that same year her short story, 'The Axe', was shortlisted for a *Times* ghost-story competition. Almost forty years since graduating from Oxford, a new phase in her life and writing career had begun.

Public recognition came quickly when, four years later, *The*

Bookshop was shortlisted for the Booker Prize. Prior to that Fitzgerald published two biographies, *Edward Burne-Jones* and *The Knox Brothers*, and her first novel or 'mystery', *The Golden Child*. As many writers did in this period, Fitzgerald then produced a novel a year for the next three years: *The Bookshop* was followed by *Offshore*, which won the Booker Prize in 1979, followed in turn by *Human Voices* (1980). Thereafter she wrote a book every other year: *At Freddie's* (1982), a third biography, *Charlotte Mew and Her Friends* (1984), *Innocence* (1986), and *The Beginning of Spring* (1988), her third novel shortlisted for the Booker Prize. It was only in 1987, aged 70, and by then a recognized figure in the English literary scene – in demand as a judge of literary prizes, speaker in schools and especially as a book reviewer – that Fitzgerald felt able finally to give up teaching. Between 1980 and 2000 she wrote over 200 book reviews for numerous publications, and two more novels appeared in the 1990s: *The Gate of Angels* (1990), the fourth time she was shortlisted for the Booker, and *The Blue Flower* (1995). *The Means of Escape*, a collection of Fitzgerald's short stories, was published shortly after her death in 2000. This was followed by a collection of her critical writing, *A House of Air* (2003), her letters, *So I Have Thought of You* (2008), and five years later by Hermione Lee's *Penelope Fitzgerald: A Life*.

Lee's biography deepens our understanding of the relationship between Fitzgerald's life and writing. It reveals the shaping of her literary sensibility by her intellectual and artistic education (English at Oxford, reviewing for *Punch* and *World Review*, scriptwriting for the BBC); her interests and heroes (English and European literature and art, belief and unbelief, Victoriana, Georgian poetry, John Ruskin, William Morris and George MacDonald, among many others); and by the Knox family culture. One recent critic has attributed the assuredness and authority of Fitzgerald's narrative voice to her upbringing as part of this eminent, well-connected family: 'she proceeds with utmost confidence that she will be heard and that we will listen, even to her reticence'.[8] In its exploration of Fitzgerald's intellectual and artistic formation, Lee's biography presents Fitzgerald not as a quintessentially English novelist, comparable with contemporaries such as Barbara Pym or Beryl Bainbridge, but as someone more usefully compared – in sensibility, style and subject matter – to European writers of short fiction, such as Turgenev, Alain-Fournier and Cesare Pavese. That is not to say that Fitzgerald's irony, realism and taste for the macabre doesn't share a great deal with other late twentieth-century British novelists such as Pym or Bainbridge or Angus Wilson or A. L. Barker. Yet there is a crucial difference of outlook. The desire of writers such as Pym, Bainbridge, Wilson or Barker to surprise or disillusion the reader arises chiefly as a reaction to hackneyed images of Englishness. Seen in the context of European short fiction, however, Fitzgerald's more profound pessimism, presented as comedy, derives from a perspective that is both more philosophically engaged and more pervasively at odds with conventional pieties.

Yet still the question remains, how precisely does she do it? How does Fitzgerald achieve 'the simultaneous compression of language and expansion of meaning', referred to by Tom Stoppard when speaking of Shakespeare? Or, put more simply, what produces in the reader of Fitzgerald's fiction the strange but invigorating feeling of 'having whisky with my tea'?[9] Part of the answer lies in the pre-eminent status Fitzgerald accords to wit, that mode of thought and expression so essential to her writing: 'Wit means self-concealment, meiosis, self-deprecation, a recognition that things are too desperate to be comic but not serious enough to be tragic, a successful attempt to make language (and silence) take charge of the situation.'[10] Wit, for Fitzgerald, is *the* principal instrument by which the human condition is comprehended in a writer's language (and silence). In this conception, wit is not simply the name given to saying sparkling things in an amusing way, though it is sometimes this too, but more profoundly, the means by which human agency itself is exercised through the apt association of thought and expression, producing surprise.[11] Another, related part of the answer lies in Fitzgerald's method of composition, the means by which the writer achieves wit on the page, researching every detail of a book's subject, then writing and rewriting, paring down to the fewest words possible: the 'endless work, on old envelopes, losing bits'.[12] Compression is a guiding principle: 'I do leave a lot out and trust the reader really to be able to understand it. [My books are] about twice the length...when they're first finished, but I cut all of it out. It's just an insult to explain everything.'[13] To understand this method further means working both inwards from the surface of Fitzgerald's writing – noting the crucial importance of the telling detail, timing, allusion, omission and highly inventive yet scarcely noticeable uses of free indirect speech – and outwards from the archival evidence of Fitzgerald's own notebooks, drafts and working papers. Held at the Harry Ransom Research Center, University of Texas at Austin, Fitzgerald's working papers reveal the fascinating ways in which she compressed, digested and distilled pages of research into her understated, enigmatic fictions. Having worked up a longhand draft in blue ink, Fitzgerald sent the manuscript to be typed professionally, before making further corrections in ink with a copy-editor's eye for grammar, syntax, spelling and presentation, adding and subtracting commas in particular to fine-tune the rhythm and modulation of the prose.[14] The apparent simplicity of Fitzgerald's writing was achieved, then, only after a lengthy process of drafting, editing and revision.

Fitzgerald's magic, however, lies not just in the technicalities of writing. It also lies in the way, as Dean Flower puts it, that her writing moves quietly 'to a deeper level where skill and moral quality, form and spiritual value, are inseparable'.[15] This move is underpinned by Fitzgerald's sense of the moral purpose of all art, about which she wrote from her earliest days. In 1953, for example, she notes with approval the moment when David Siquerios, the Mexican social realist artist, 'first perceived the social duty of the painter'.[16] Later in life, Fitzgerald summed up her personal sense of this moral purpose: 'I have remained true to my deepest convictions – I mean to the courage of those who are born to be defeated, the weaknesses of the strong, and the tragedy of misunderstandings and missed opportunities which I have done my best to treat as a comedy, for otherwise how can we manage to bear it?' (*HA* 480). Closely linked to this moral understanding of art – A. S. Byatt called it 'a religious understanding of the individual, which gives shape to Penelope Fitzgerald's novels' – is Fitzgerald's passionate sense of fiction as a sort of compensation for the hardness of life, especially of women's lives: 'Women, if they possibly can, *must* write novels, covering the irritations of every day with a fine, iridescent coating of art.'[17] It is a priority of this present book, then, to foreground Fitzgerald's moral sense, forged by family, predilection and her historical moment, for later generations of readers whose experiences and encounters with language and literature and their relationship to the world have been and will be shaped, in most cases, by quite different kinds of conditions and pressures.

Six chapters follow. Three shorter chapters examine Fitzgerald's writing as a critic and reviewer, biographer, short-story writer, letter-writer and poet. Two longer chapters explore the style and contexts of her early and late novels. A concluding chapter considers her literary reputation and influence. In all of them I aim to distinguish between the *effects* created by Fitzgerald's writing and the *means* by which those effects are achieved. In making this distinction, I frequently apply Fitzgerald's critical judgments about other writers to her own work. She is, more often than not, her own best critic. To give one example: in a review of a biography of George Eliot, Fitzgerald wrote that Eliot considered, in her best writing, that 'there was a "not-herself" which took possession' (*HA* 39). It is difficult, as Fitzgerald concedes, to write a story of a not-herself, but that is what accounts of a writer should at least aim to provide, and I also try to do that here. This is a short book, in keeping with the economy and restraint of its subject. In a review written for *Punch* in 1942 of Graham Greene's *British Dramatists* and Rose Macaulay's *Life Among the English*, both introductory guides to their subjects, Fitzgerald observes: 'The best you can do in a ten-thousand-word essay on an unwieldy subject is to flatter the readers by supposing they know something about it, be brilliant, and since you cannot be comprehensive, stick firmly to your personal prejudices.'[18] I have tried, without apology, to follow this advice, making this, I hope, a livelier if not entirely dispassionate sort of essay. If, by its end, the reader turns to Fitzgerald's writing for the first time, or returns to it with a new way of reading, this book will have succeeded in its aims.

1

Critical Writing

Penelope Fitzgerald's career as a literary critic started young. At school she wrote reviews of plays and lectures for the *Wycombe Abbey Gazette*, and at Oxford she provided short pieces on the arts for *Isis* and *Cherwell*, the two main University newspapers.[1] In her twenties, Fitzgerald contributed more than fifty book, film and theatre reviews for *Punch*, and in her early thirties she wrote or co-wrote more than twenty essays on European art, literature and culture for *World Review*, the short-lived periodical that she edited with her husband Desmond. In the last two decades of her life, after she had won the Booker Prize and become well-known, she wrote more than two hundred reviews of fiction and biography for the *London Review of Books*, *Times Literary Supplement*, *New York Times Book Review* and other British and American newspapers and journals, as well as introductions for books and editions, travel essays, art criticism, literary essays and journalistic sketches.[2] This is an impressive volume of work by any measure, only a relatively small selection of which has been collected and is currently in print, in *House of Air* (2003). Because Fitzgerald's reputation is chiefly as a novelist and biographer, very little to date has been said about this body of critical writing, despite what it reveals about the cosmopolitan range and depth of her intellectual and artistic sympathies, enduring attitudes and priorities in her work (such as the central places held by humour, stoicism and emotion), and the marked stylistic continuities between her criticism and fiction. This chapter considers the nature of these critical sympathies, priorities and tastes, and their significance for Fitzgerald's fiction, by examining selected examples of Fitzgerald's writing from *Punch*, *World Review* and her later book reviews and critical essays.

Time and again in her criticism Fitzgerald meditates on what would become two of the most distinctive features of her own writing: a searching appreciation of the emotional, psychological and social interplay between fictional characters, and a prose style apparently without art. In 1952 Fitzgerald observed of Alberto Moravia's *The Conformist*:

> His control is astonishing, in particular his power of maintaining interest in several characters, each of whom reacts upon and modifies the others.... In this, and in the plainness and ease of his style (it is criticised in Italy as an absence of style) Moravia is a school for novelists.[3]

Fitzgerald's interest in the way that people 'react upon and modify' each other underpins all of her novels. The same interest is manifestly evident in her earliest critical writing. In a 1942 *Punch* review of *Macbeth*, with John Gielgud and Gwen Ffrangcon-Davies, Fitzgerald spells out the emotional logic of the play:

> as one descends, the other ascends. While he doubts, she gives him strength. When he is infirm of purpose, she takes the daggers.... This ascending and descending balance is *the* balance of the play, and it is a producer's business to see to the weights.[4]

This observation of the delicate interplay between characters, its ascending and descending balance, which would become in time *the* balance of Fitzgerald's novels, is everywhere in Fitzgerald's early criticism. In *Punch* reviews of the 1940s Fitzgerald praises the Austrian novelist Vicki Baum's 'mastery of emotional scenes', Elizabeth Bowen's 'hair's-breadth dissection of motive', and Elizabeth Taylor's 'penetration into different minds', which 'has made her write all her novels, not from a single viewpoint, but slipping rapidly in and out of each character'.[5] Such fine emotional calibrations would become a distinctive feature of Fitzgerald's own fiction, yet she could also appreciate passions painted with a broader brush. Discussing the extravagantly rebellious personality of the Italian sculptor Medardo Rosso, Fitzgerald evokes an image from the war in heaven in Book 6 of Milton's *Paradise Lost* when the angels tear up whole mountains and hurl them at one another: 'Even his ferocious quarrel with Rodin, after their earlier amity and exchange of gifts, was on a giant scale, as though weighty fragments of stone and bronze were moving through the air.'[6] This example provides a foretaste of the discreet allusiveness of Fitzgerald's fiction in general, while also suggesting a link with one of Fitzgerald's characters in particular. More than a hint of Rosso's explosive temper (and surname) survives in the hero of *Innocence*, Salvatore Rossi.

Readers of Fitzgerald's novels will not be surprised by her admiration for 'the plainness and ease' of Moravia's writing. Fitzgerald's criticism, however, deepens our sense of her technical appreciation of prose style. Her review of Lionel Trilling's *E. M. Forster* picks up on counterpoint as the essence of Forster's art: the apparent paradox that Forster is out to show us that the one thing worth having is richness of life, but that he does so 'in a gentle, retiring, unassuming style, so delicate as to be almost dry'.[7] As so often in Fitzgerald's critical writing, this analysis is neatly self-reflexive, applying just as much to her own prose style as to Forster's. Elsewhere, Fitzgerald explores the sources, kinds and purposes of plainness of style. The debt to orality is fundamental: 'English is, and always will be, as she is spoken.'[8] To illustrate, Fitzgerald approvingly quotes poet and short-story writer A. E. Coppard's 'homely' (though not basic) style: 'The widow's last man had hung himself on a plum-tree, and that's a cold warning to any bachelor.' ... 'The clock of time ticks you off, it ticks you off, and although Thaniel's hour had not yet struck he was being put, and not very gently either, on one side.' There's a palpable delight here, both in Coppard and Fitzgerald, in the grotesque aspect of plain style that Fitzgerald identifies as peculiarly English, 'recognizable from every country lane, rectory, pub and doorstep'.[9] Plainness or ease of style is also entirely compatible with, and indeed is conducive to, sharp observations, as Fitzgerald acknowledges in her appreciative quotation of two war-time examples of novelist and critic G. W. Stonier's 'indestructible' wit: 'What a masterly touch too in the hotel where meals are eaten "with cold thoroughness," or the conversation through the bathroom door "like a trunk call to a Channel swimmer".'[10] Nor does ease of style prohibit linguistic exuberance. In a 1944 *Punch* review, Fitzgerald rejoices in the style of Jack Yeats (who wrote articles for *Punch* under the pseudonym 'W. Bird'), whose reminiscences 'pour out in a golden stream of words, full of hidden allusions and chance snatches of verse'.[11]

Fitzgerald's own style in her critical writing contains aspects of all of these qualities. Aphoristic wit, later so essential to her fiction, conveys both humour and authority: 'A good moral... is said to improve the digestion, and this, with Tamiroff's fine acting, makes the film worth visiting.'[12] Pretensions are gently deflated: 'the root of the trouble is that the play requires the whole cast to talk about the eternal verities, and they don't seem used to it'.[13] Character is weighed in the balance – of Olive Schreiner Fitzgerald observes:

> Her letters show her courage, her integrity, and her intuition, and, with them, the alarming neurotic force of the Victorian 'wonder woman'. It was this, probably, that made the liberal politician J. X. Merriman call her 'one of those persons one admires more at a distance'.[14]

Merriman's sardonic remark elicits from the reader a smile of recognition, but it is Fitzgerald's deftly weighted use of the modifier 'probably' that saves the reader from leaping to judgment, enabling him or her both to admire *and* be alarmed by Schreiner at the same time.

Fitzgerald's critical writing also shows her keen sense of rhetorical decorum, adapting her style according to subject matter and genre. In a review of a book on fairs, circuses and music halls, Fitzgerald implicitly asserts this rhetorical principle, lamenting the author's dryly academic treatment of his subject: 'Erudition is an admirable thing, but it won't jump through paper hoops, paw the ground, or be sold at three goes for twopence.... We don't feel *endimanchés*.'[15] By contrast, Fitzgerald's own critical writing adopts the style or mode most in keeping with the subject matter reviewed. Praising the sepia visuals of *The Westerner*, Fitzgerald writes:

> Gary Cooper is handsomer than ever in shades of daguerrotype buff and brown; the horses, the homesteads, the saloon bar, are rounded off with melting shadows; the bad sheriff, whose heart is of gold, has a face of bronze; six-shooters seem to explode harmlessly in the sepia air, hooves seem muffled, and the brown cornfields rest the ear – the golden ear, Pope's rather odd phrase, really does embrown the slope – and even the great fire seems made of chocolate.[16]

Such moments of resonant lyricism in Fitzgerald's critical writing, enriched by literary allusion, prefigure similarly pictorial tableaux in brief passages on nature in her novels: the description, taken from Whistler, of the Thames at dusk in *Offshore*, 'when evening mist clothes the riverside with poetry, as with a veil' (*OF* 38); or, in a different key, the midday glare in the fields at Valsassina in *Innocence*: 'Outside, the ragged sky burned like a blue and white fire, hard on the eyes' (*IN* 25). It is a critical commonplace that Fitzgerald's handling of comic irony bears comparison with that of Jane Austen, but there is nothing in Austen like this stylistic flexibility – stepping briskly outdoors, as it were, from the comedy of manners.

As well as being appreciative of emotional intelligence and ease of style, Fitzgerald's critical writing returns again and again to the importance of meticulous observation and invention. A 1940 *Punch* review of Carol Reed's *Night Train to Munich* praises its 'neat and ingenious details. Watch out for the moment when the note is hidden under the doughnut, for the German station-mistress, and for a delightful moment in the gentlemen's cloakroom.'[17] George Simenon's 'clinical realism' is admired, as 'Step by step he follows his characters, without compassion, registering even the grease on an hotel arm-chair or a burnt-out matchstick. It is a paralysing, fascinating method, like a bird watching a snake.'[18] Fitzgerald counts the number of bullets fired in westerns and spy thrillers (and is often disappointed: 'Fred MacMurray...dispatches them in very few revolver shots – I doubt, in fact if they get one apiece').[19] She admires an author's 'scrupulous notice of small details (the dark green tin vases in the churchyards, the paper hats in crackers, "fragile, rakish, creased and unbecoming", the dolls' tea-sets...)',[20] and rejoices in the recollection of a long-forgotten item of clothing: '"Afterwards, most of the men took off their jackets, exposing their braces and the tapes of their long woollen underpants, and astonished their children by larking around like great lads." Those tapes! Who would have remembered them except Jim Carr?'[21] Contemporary female novelists of the 1940s, such as Elizabeth Taylor, Elizabeth Bowen, Elizabeth Jenkins, Stella Gibbons and Betty Miller, are praised for their 'acute relish for the appearance of things, dwelling lovingly on what can be touched, stared at and smelt'.[22]

But the accumulation of detail is never simply for its own sake. Rather, it is part of a larger recipe for creating an imagined world, as Fitzgerald observes of Cecil Beaton, praising, 'His eye for detail, for good stories, for atmosphere and above all colour'.[23] Details of the physical environment establish the realistic setting within which fantastical, absurd or grotesque events take place: 'nothing is more pathetic or sinister in a scene of violence than a quite familiar, or even exceedingly ordinary object'. Examples in Alfred Hitchcock's *Foreign Correspondent* include: 'buses, railway refreshment-rooms, theatres, pierrots at the seaside, Sunday dinner, church services, lunch at Simpsons', music halls and third-class carriages'. Fitzgerald the cinemagoer relishes the moment of violence when it comes: it makes 'your blood run cold, and the sensation of blood running cold in an overheated cinema is, as everyone knows, a pleasant one, much like eating ice-cream with hot chocolate sauce'.[24] Fitzgerald carries this delight in the coupling of the grotesque and ordinary into her novels, in striking images such as the murder of Sir William in *The Golden Child*, trapped between sliding shelf units in the Staff Library, and the flesh of Nisbet's arm 'sucked off to the last shreds' by nuns in *The Gate of Angels* (173). Such gratifyingly macabre moments are often foreshadowed in Fitzgerald's articles for *World Review* in the 1950s. A piece on Spanish painted sculpture relishes the lengths to which the artist Francisco Salzillo would go in the name of art: 'Salzillo is supposed to have burst in on his wife and announced that their eldest son was dead, simply in order to study her expression for his *Dolorosa*.'[25] An article on Mexican art revels in grisly detail: 'The Aztecs ate parts of the corpses and carefully dissected others... the faces of their priests were painted black, and, in that cleanly city, they were never allowed to wash their hair, which was matted with endless soakings of blood.'[26] It is no distance at all from here to the strangulation of Waring Smith with (fake) golden twine in *The Golden Child*, or the blinding and amputations of *Innocence*, or the bear cub on fire in *The Beginning of Spring*.

Important as they are, details are only one part of the story. Fitzgerald's critical writing attends to *all* aspects of the novelist's craft, and many of her remarks illuminate her own practice. On narrative voice, Fitzgerald applauds Vicki Baum's 'occasional touches of insight which persuade you against your better judgement, that these characters are real'.[27] On plot, Fitzgerald notes those of A. E. Coppard's tales that seem to say of themselves, 'there is occasionally a little more than at first meets the eye, buried lightly as it were. It can't be helped, that's the way it goes'.[28] Almost forty years later, Fitzgerald honoured the place of plot in novels:

> In the novel's domain, plots were the earliest and the poorest relations to arrive. For the last two hundred years there have been repeated attempts to get them to leave, or at least to confine themselves to satire, fantasy, and dream. Picaresque novels, however, both old and new, are a kind of gesture towards them, acknowledging that although you can easily spend your whole life wandering about, you can't do so in a book without recurrent coincidences and, after all, a return. And the readers of books like plots. That, too, is worth consideration. (*HA* 498)

The continuity of ideas and opinions between Fitzgerald's earlier criticism, in the 1940s and 1950s, when she thought that she would one day become a novelist, and her later critical writing, in the 1980s and after, when she had done so, is striking. Touches of insight that persuade us the fiction is real, plots with more going on than at first meets the eye, and the inevitability that a novel's end will return to its beginning: Fitzgerald picks out those things in the novels of others that most distinguish her own.

In all of her reviews, essays and articles Fitzgerald pays particularly close attention to the way people speak. Her 1939 *TLS* article, 'War on Wit', celebrates heightened realism in dialogue:

> It is a pity that the modern novel too often confounds realism with dullness. Perhaps no living person ever talked like Millamant, or Lord Henry, or Zuleika Dobson, or Mrs. Mountstuart Jenkinson; all the better that they do so in print! Echoes of our own boredom dissatisfy us, and it is a relief to contemplate these unruffled creatures whose tongues cannot slip and whose casual remarks are alarming in their neatness.[29]

Written when Fitzgerald was just twenty-two, this early satirical intervention is interesting not only for the light it sheds on her sensibility as a budding novelist, but as a piece of criticism in its own right: it displays Fitzgerald's lifelong concern with the effect that written speech has on the emotions ('dissatisfied', 'relieved', 'alarmed') as much as the intellect. As Fitzgerald was well aware, a fine line separates witty talk and something altogether more knowing and brittle. Ronald Fraser's novel, *The Fiery Gate*, is criticized for 'a wealth of smart dialogue which makes one long, unlike Alice, for a book without conversations'.[30] By contrast, Louis MacNeice's radio play, *Christopher Columbus*, is praised for its 'true understanding of the counterpoint of the human voice. Addison, who liked to compare conversation to an orchestra, would have made a good radio critic'.[31] A later essay on dialogue beautifully demonstrates the effects of switching from direct to reported speech: 'The storyteller's instinct, or perhaps his judgement, tells him when they have gone on long enough to make their greatest impact, and when to let the voices fall silent.' Fitzgerald illustrates her remark with an example from *Pickwick Papers*. '"I say, old boy, where do you hang out?" Mr Pickwick replied that he was at present suspended at the George and Vulture.' She comments: 'If Dickens had made Pickwick say "I am at present suspended &c &c" the effect would be gone, vanished into the vast limbo of failed ironies' (HA 501, 506). By contrast, Pickwick's ironical good humour is preserved and at the same time made more interestingly ambiguous by reported speech: is his pun on 'suspended' mocking the questioner's slang enquiry, or meeting it on its own terms? Whether reported or direct, speech must always serve the larger aims of the story: 'I have to try to see to it that every confrontation and every dialogue has some reference to what I hope will be understood as the heart of the novel. As I've tried to explain, it's about body, mind, and spirit' (HA 517). This is an important reminder of where Fitzgerald's priorities lay, as both critic and novelist: craft and technique are vital insofar as they relate to the central task of representing in words what it feels like, sensually, mentally and spiritually, to be alive.

Fitzgerald's critical views on poetry, about which she wrote often for *Punch*, can also help us to understand and appreciate her fiction. Lyricism, musicality and emotion are preferred ingredients. Fitzgerald praises Frederic Prokosch for his 'true inward ear for the vowel sounds of the English language' and his ability to write 'the simple melodies which are some of the most difficult of all'.[32] Walter de la Mare, in 1945, 'still has the best musical ear of any living writer – sensitive to the faintest echo, the least drip or fall of sound'. 'His world has always been a place of immense, disquieting solitudes.'[33] T. S. Eliot's descriptive epithets in *Four Quartets* are also commended: '*Little Gidding* has two, "Ash on an old man's sleeve" and "The dove descending breaks the air," which have a pure singing tone as true as anything he has ever written.'[34] Fitzgerald writes appreciatively too of Louis MacNeice: his 'sardonic gift and his almost morbid fear of anything that is too easy have repaid him a hundredfold'.[35] In the Greek poet C. P. Cavafy she appreciates, above all, the variety of his expressions of emotional states: 'He is a writer of anti-climaxes, of uncomfortable irony and disconcerting echoes, but in his love-poems he is agonisingly direct and clear.'[36] Fitzgerald's remarks about Cavafy in 1951 could equally apply, three decades later, to her own fiction; her commitment to emotional directness, clarity and the 'uncomfortable irony' of what is not said persisted throughout her entire writing career.

The reverse side of the coin was Fitzgerald's more ambivalent response to the often recondite complexities of literary symbolism, whether in poetry or prose. In a 1943 *Punch* review, Fitzgerald attempted to explicate Eliot's theory in *Four Quartets* of the unimportance of Time, of the symbolic equivalence of the moment of the rose and the moment of the yew tree, the fusion of each moment with eternity, and our source in God. Fitzgerald concludes:

> It is not an easy idea and Eliot has never been good at explaining things clearly. You regret this when reading his critical essays, but not in his poetry.... There are still the echoes, the literary allusions (some very unexpected ones), and it is for you to decide whether these really enrich the poetry or whether they are more like a nightmare parlour-game, with the other side making up all the rules.[37]

The appreciation here of echoes and literary allusions is a constant in Fitzgerald's writing about poetry in the 1940s, as is her impatience with poetry that merely appears to play games. She complains of Stephen Spender's *Poems of Dedication* that Spender asks 'language to do what it will not do – the art of the crossword-puzzle, not of poetry'; 'the language has been so carefully refined, worked out, worked to death, that the human sorrow appears only in flashes'.[38] A year later, reviewing Louis

MacNeice's *Holes in the Sky*, she summarizes the problem as she sees it, referring to the era of Auden, Day-Lewis, Spender and MacNeice: 'First the 'twenties, now the 'thirties, slide away and become a literary period – a period of schoolmasters turned poets, and poets inexorably, cleverly and drily turned schoolmasters.'[39] Poetry of the lamp, fed only on a diet of booklearning rather than anything more nourishing, was always a target for Fitzgerald's wit. Of Sidney Keyes, she says that 'he was still in bondage to the symbolists – to Yeats, to T. S. Eliot, and above all to Rilke; Rilke, one of the giant invalids of modern literature, tortured by the noise of traffic, shut off from life in his tower or in the Bibliothèque Nationale, dying at last from the prick of a rose'.[40] Yet Fitzgerald the critic was always fair-minded. Edith Sitwell she calls 'the most gracious of the modern symbolists', and concludes: 'You may say this is artificial; but you will recognize the rare combination of a feeling heart and exquisitely cultivated mind.'[41] In an editorial article on Herman Melville's *Billy Budd*, though critical of Melville's heavy underlining of his symbolism, Fitzgerald adds: 'But at least he has the courage to sustain it to its illogical conclusion.'[42] Courage, a feeling heart, truthfulness: these are the human qualities that redeem poetry or fiction for Fitzgerald, even when their modes of expression are not to her taste.

Above all, Fitzgerald admired craftsmanship, whether in writing, the visual or manual arts. In her article on Spanish painted sculpture she observed: 'The manual arts give the deepest satisfaction of all but none deeper, surely, than a lifetime of creating living images out of the living wood.'[43] Reviewing Thomas Hennell's *British Craftsmen*, Fitzgerald praises Hennell's 'knowledge and affection for good workmanship and the raw material itself as when he calculates that the weight of a Tudor roof on its timbers is less than their native load of "twig, leaf and acorn"'.[44] As well as technical skill, the craftsman should possess dedication, sincerity and an awareness of his or her social duty. The poet George Barker's 'sincerity is almost frightening.... It does not matter that he is sometimes unlucky with words, or forced and irritating, because beyond all question he is a poet and language is his art'.[45] Different writers, Fitzgerald acknowledged, held different conceptions of the function of literature: 'While Tolstoy and William Morris both came to doubt art's power to change society – and if it failed in that it failed for them in everything – James Joyce and Virginia Woolf entrusted themselves to it, for its own sake, entirely' (*HA* 530). When Fitzgerald thought of her own attitude to writing, it was the image of the skilled, socially committed and useful craftsman, combining a vocational sense and equal measure of idealism and pragmatism, which appealed to her most. '1. [I write] because something inside me compels me to tell stories; 2. I am drawn to people who seem to have been born defeated or, even, profoundly lost; 3. I write to make money. In a world full of dangers it is comforting to be considered, even wrongly, a crafty so-and-so' (*HA* 508–9).

Penelope Fitzgerald's critical writing is the continuous thread that runs through her sixty-year writing career, from young Oxford journalist to prize-winning octogenarian novelist. When contributing reviews to *Punch* in the 1940s she rubbed literary shoulders with British luminaries such as E. H. Shepard, Basil Boothroyd, E. M. Delafield, Lord Dunsany, Joyce Grenfell, A. A. Milne, Jan Struther, Geoffrey Willans and P. G. Wodehouse. Fitzgerald's characteristic wit and reticence undoubtedly owes a debt to the *Punch* house style. Hugh Kingsmill, a senior staff-writer in the 1940s, wrote of Edmund Blunden's biography of Thomas Hardy: 'This book is one of those blameless critical studies that dilute genius to a strength at which it can be absorbed without risk by the weakest stomach.'[46] Fitzgerald's reviews of the same period sound a similar note of urbane understatement, yet in the service of a more generous and resonant appreciation of literary beauty. In the 1950s, Fitzgerald's reviews and editorial articles for *World Review* appeared alongside writing by a remarkable international roster of literary talent: Bertrand Russell, J. D. Salinger, Albert Camus, Louis MacNeice, Patrick Leigh-Fermor, Stevie Smith, Walter de la Mare, John Betjeman, Henry Miller, V. S. Pritchett, Bernard Malamud, André Malraux, Karl Jaspers, Osbert Sitwell, Muriel Spark, Alberto Moravia, Dylan Thomas, Cyril Connolly, Giorgio Bassani and Norman Mailer.[47] Few novelists writing four decades later, if any, could claim quite such an illustrious literary apprenticeship.

Undoubtedly, Fitzgerald's artistic tastes, sensibility and writing style – in many ways, though not all – trace their roots to her childhood and the Knox family culture. Yet it was in these years, from 1937 to 1953, reviewing for *Punch*, scriptwriting for the BBC, editing and writing for *World Review*, that she came of age as a writer. So many of the virtues of her later biographical, fictional and critical writing – the slyly subversive wit, passionate emotions kept beneath the surface, the feeling for the downtrodden, and the reticent yet authoritative narrative voice – were ones possessed more generally by writers of the 1940s and early 50s. Literary fashions and attitudes change, and yet, ironically, the success Fitzgerald's writing found from 1979 on may well have owed an unexpected debt to the social and cultural upheaval of the previous decade. Modern readers turning to Fitzgerald's books heard with relief and a feeling close to nostalgia the authentic voice of an earlier era. For some it was the voice of their parents – for others, their grandparents. Fitzgerald herself hadn't changed but the times had, and later readers appreciated all the more those qualities in her writing that earlier readers might well have taken for granted.

2

Biographies

Penelope Fitzgerald published three group biographies – *Edward Burne-Jones* (1975), *The Knox Brothers* (1977) and *Charlotte Mew and Her Friends* (1984) – and began, but eventually gave up, a life of the novelist L. P. Hartley. Over six decades she also reviewed and wrote introductions for numerous writers' lives, ranging from canonical figures such as S. T. Coleridge, George Eliot and Virginia Woolf to less well-remembered novelists, poets and artists such as Margaret Oliphant, John Lehmann and C. R. Ashbee.[1] Fitzgerald believed from the beginning that the biographer's attitude to her subject should be one of love and respect. In 1945 she reviewed Edwin Honig's *Garcia Lorca* for *Punch*, observing: 'Clearly he loved his subject, this side idolatry, and there is no better basis for biography.'[2] More than thirty years later, by then an accomplished biographer in her own right, she still felt the same: 'A primary biography by people who know the subject and are really fond of him or her is a protection, I think.'[3] She knew just how demanding a biographer's task could be, and towards the end of her life doubted that she still had the energy and perseverance required.[4] Yet Fitzgerald never lost her belief that biography could achieve a profound and intimate understanding of its subject: 'It seems to me that (particularly if you have the letters, and if you knew the subject yourself or can get hold of someone who knew the subject) you can know him or her at least as well as anyone you meet in real life.'[5] Fitzgerald's biographies (and especially *The Knox Brothers*) provide important clues to the distinctive sensibility we find in her novels. In particular, Fitzgerald's biographies show that no one can be understood without taking his or her family, friends and colleagues into consideration. The same view holds in Fitzgerald's novels, where joy, pain and everything in between depend almost wholly on the ties that bind.

EDWARD BURNE-JONES (1975)

Fitzgerald's first biography, about the lives and work of the Victorian artists and craftsmen Edward Burne-Jones ('Ned') and William Morris ('Top'), and Ned's wife, Georgiana Burne-Jones ('Georgie'), arose from her longstanding fascination with the art, culture and social worlds of mid-nineteenth-century England. Her interest in Burne-Jones and Morris, the Arts and Crafts movement and the medieval revival was sparked early, having been taken as a child to see the stained-glass window of the Last Judgement designed by Burne-Jones for Birmingham Cathedral (*PF* 216). The values that underpinned Ned and Top's work – craft, beauty, honesty, imagination, the inner life, collective spirit, the transformative power of art – were the same ones that drove and excited hers. Many of the finest qualities of *Edward Burne-Jones* – deft handling of masses of research, the vivid evocation of a distinct time, place and community, and the ability to cut to the emotional or spiritual heart of the matter through the accretion of minutely observed detail – are characteristic features of both her fiction and non-fiction.

Fitzgerald's technical appreciation of Burne-Jones's art is the foundation upon which the life is written. Her analysis of the painting, *Green Summer*, offers a typical example. In three concise paragraphs Fitzgerald explains the painting's outward form ('an arrangement of greens in light and shadow... as though Giorgione had come to Abbey Woods in Kent'), its personal reference (the 'central figures are variations on the Macdonald sisters'), its title (an echo of a passage in *Morte d'Arthur*: 'How true love is likened to summer'), and its 'burden', a term appropriated by Ned to indicate the intrinsic meaning of a thing, awaiting understanding by an attentive viewer. 'The burden of *Green Summer* is beauty guilty of its own mortality' (*EB* 93). The social and cultural world which Ned and Morris inhabited, in which they lived, loved, drew, designed and painted, is portrayed as packed with people, places, events and things: 'We catch glimpses of Burne-Jones playing dominoes with Lord Salisbury, or taking Oscar Wilde home in a four-wheeler when he was "the saddest man in London". Sarah Bernhardt and Paderewski came to the studio' (*EB* 230).

Fitzgerald's account of the art of the period is underpinned by her understanding of the Victorian concept of myth, encapsulated in Malory's *Morte d'Arthur*, painted by Dante Gabriel Rossetti and Burne-Jones and interpreted by John Ruskin and Walter Pater. Pater referred to the 'latent capability' of the story. But a myth's power and resonance is not simply a matter of its universality. 'The myth is only alive if it is the image of individual experience, and as Ruskin says, if we have "the material in our own minds for an intelligent answering sympathy"' (*EB* 120). This comes close to Fitzgerald's understanding in her own work of the collaborative relationship between artist and audience, writer and reader, and it is significant that Ned and Morris were turned into artists by reading books (in particular, Kenelm Digby's *The Broadstone of Honour*, De La Motte Fouqué's *Sintram* and Charlotte Yonge's *The Heir of Redclyffe*). Fitzgerald paraphrases her touchstone, Ruskin, from his study of Athena, Greek goddess of wisdom: ' You cannot make a myth unless you have something to make it of. You cannot tell a secret you don't know...if the sunrise is a daily restoration and the purging of fear by the baptism of the dew, only then shall we understand the sun myth.' But she adds, in a typically glancing touch of her own: 'And only if we are afraid to lose a daughter shall we understand *Briar Rose*' (*EB* 199).[6]

As in her other biographies, Fitzgerald brings a novelist's attention to the emotional and imaginative lives of her subjects. Burne-Jones, who lost his mother a few days after his birth, and his sister in infancy, was the son of a hard-working but unsuccessful Birmingham gilder and frame-maker. It was, Burne-Jones said, 'a childhood without beauty', and the poverty and hunger he saw all about him in 1830s Birmingham led to a lifelong concern with human suffering and 'uneasy craving for beauty' (*EB* 16, 19). Fitzgerald is tolerant, or at least understanding, of one of the consequences of that craving – Ned's habit of falling in love, repeatedly, with women who weren't his wife (including, most damagingly, Maria Zambaco, but also Frances Graham and May Gaskell).[7] Passionate natures need only the smallest cue for invention and imagination, and Ned was no exception. Fitzgerald portrays him as a schoolboy at King Edward's Free School enraptured by his teacher's flights of free association: 'he would take us to ocean waters and the marshes of Babylon... and the constellations and abysses of space'. What saves Fitzgerald's account from sentimentality is her comic irony, gently and deflatingly expressed: '[Ned] noticed, however, as he listened to Mr Thompson's fantasies in word-derivation, that the master was sometimes drunk' (*EB* 18).

How people speak is a matter of constant fascination and delight, here and in all of Fitzgerald's writing. Rossetti's mid-nineteenth-century London slang – 'spiffy', 'jammy', 'spoony', 'nobble', 'ticker' and 'stock-dolloger' (for a knock-down blow) – is complemented by phrases peculiar to the Macdonald household (the family of Ned's wife Georgie): unhappiness was 'the screws', a nap a 'modest quencher', and the resonant family proverb, immediately understood by Ned, was: 'Bare is back without brother behind' (*EB* 47, 52). The symbolic language of images, particularly of flowers, now largely forgotten, which speaks so insistently in Ned's paintings, interested Fitzgerald intensely throughout her life. 'The final version of *Briar Rose* was the culmination of flower languages – the "burden" of the thorn and the rose' (*EB* 225). At Ned's funeral in 1898 there were lilies of the valley. 'Georgie also brought flowers to be carried to the grave – a small wreath of hearts-ease' (*EB* 284).

Everything Fitzgerald held dear in life and art can be found in *Edward Burne-Jones*. Craftsmanship, skill and labour are rated far above hollow intellectualism or politicking. Fitzgerald quotes Ned: 'A man who is a good carpenter is well educated, and man who can smithy a horseshoe is well educated, and man who knows what other people have said about these things is not well educated at all' (*EB* 204). Ruskin, in his Edinburgh lectures championing the Pre-Raphaelite Brotherhood, had praised their technical superiority, enormous care and labour, and uncompromising moral truth. Ned accepted the first two of these attributes but not the third. 'What he knew from his own experience was that beauty is an essential element without which human nature is diminished. If art gives us beauty it will make us more like human beings' (*EB* 30-1). This belief in 'the land that is more true than real' (*EB* 226) over morality, politics or other social virtues is one that Fitzgerald shared with her heroes, Burne-Jones, Morris and Ruskin. She recounts Ned's brief flirtation with moral causes when he sided with Gladstone's liberal arguments on the Eastern Question of 1876. Fitzgerald tersely records Ned's initial enthusiasm, followed by disillusion and retreat: 'For the first and last time in his life, Burne-Jones became interested in politics, and in the perpetual delusion that through political means we can better the human condition' (*EB* 162).

This is a pessimistic view, but not a fatalistic one. For Fitzgerald, as for Ned, Ruskin and Newman, the life of the spirit was the only truly transformative source of power (and particularly for Ned, 'spirituality expressed through colour' (*EB* 33)). This deeply-held sense made Ned and those who thought like him 'scorners of the world', whether they liked it or not. For Burne-Jones, 'the reality of beauty consisted of uniting the form and the spirit' (*EB* 279), and Fitzgerald too, whose paternal grandfather had been the Evangelical Bishop of Manchester, honoured the spiritual tradition throughout her life: 'It is to the credit of humanity that whenever it has been clearly put, there have always been people to attend to it' (*EB* 57).

Edward Burne-Jones is a seedbed for all of Fitzgerald's subsequent writing. The banked-down emotions and intense inner lives of Ned, Morris and Georgie reappear in different outward forms in those of *The Knox Brothers* and *Charlotte Mew and Her Friends*. William Morris may have been the model for Len Coker, the socialist craftsman in *The Golden Child*. William de Morgan's magical ceramics surface in *Offshore*. The cyclists' collision and hint of the numinous in *The Gate of Angels*, the technical accounts of the printer's craft in *The Beginning of Spring*, and the Swiss gentian at the end of *The Bookshop*, are all prefigured in Fitzgerald's first biography. Pen portraits of Thomas Carlyle, George du Maurier, Alphonse Legros, Val Prinsep, Leslie Stephen, Sidney Colvin and many others are echoed and multiplied by Fitzgerald in hundreds of character sketches in her fiction. Connections to *The Blue Flower* are particularly evident. Research on George MacDonald led Fitzgerald to Novalis (Friedrich von Hardenberg), and it is tempting to see the pious yet loving and joyous Macdonald family as a model for the Moravian Brotherhood household of the Hardenbergs. The Macdonalds' story 'is of an unworldly preacher bringing up, or rather letting his wife bring up, a large family on a tiny income...so that to buy a book or to have the piano tuned was a heroic event....Visitors who were in the least pretentious were cut short. Lord Baldwin records that a preacher who spoke of his heart as "black, and full of stones" was told by little Louie that he must mean his gizzard' (*EB* 22). One could well imagine the Bernhard in *The Blue Flower* saying the same thing in Louie's situation, and in much the same way.

Such is Fitzgerald's skill as a biographer, in selecting and weaving together the most pungent, affecting and telling anecdotes, quotations and histories, that the reader is reluctant to take leave of Burne-Jones at the end of the book. Ned's nephew, Rudyard Kipling ('Ruddie of my heart') felt deeply for his uncle, and it is to Kipling's *Kim* that Fitzgerald turns in her parting words on Burne-Jones: 'Who else', she asks, 'is the old lama, whose life is a quest which others do not understand, who can draw with pen and ink in a way that is almost lost to the world, who shows Kim his art "not for pride's sake, but because thou must learn", and who tells stories that hold him spellbound?' (*EB* 275). This Fitzgerald word portrait, as in so many others, contains more than a hint of herself.

THE KNOX BROTHERS (1977)

Appearing two years after *Edward Burne-Jones*, *The Knox Brothers* recalls the lives of Fitzgerald's father, Edmund ('E. V.' or 'Evoe' or 'Eddie') Knox, and his three brothers, Dillwyn ('Dilly'), Wilfred and Ronald ('Ronnie').[8] Born into a clerical family in the 1880s (their father, E. A. Knox, became Bishop of Manchester), the characters, tastes and eccentricities of all four boys were shaped by their rectory childhood. With her characteristic mixture of concision, pathos and wit, Fitzgerald tracks the brothers' lives, switching her narrative between them, from the early death of their mother and their father's remarriage, through their education at Rugby, Eton, Oxford and Cambridge, and on through their careers. Eddie, a poet and journalist, eventually became editor of *Punch*. Dilly, a Greek literary scholar and cryptographer, decoded enemy signals in both the First and

Second World War. Wilfred, ordained as an Anglo-Catholic minister, served as chaplain of Pembroke College, Cambridge. And Ronnie, a converted Roman Catholic priest, prolific writer on religious subjects (and, in his earlier days, of detective novels), became Oxford University's Roman Catholic chaplain, and translator of the Latin Vulgate Bible. Fitzgerald's affection for her father and uncles is palpable. In a later reprint she remarks simply: 'I miss them all more than I can say'. But she is a perceptive as well as a sympathetic observer, summing up the formative influences and preoccupations of each brother in a few brief lines: 'Eddie could never forget that he was the eldest, Dilly that he was the second, Wilfred that he was the cheerfully and necessarily philosophic third, Ronnie that he was the baby. Eddie looked for responsibility, Dilly for independence, Wilfred for reunion, Ronnie for authority. All needed love, Wilfred and Ronnie because they had so much in childhood, Eddie and Dilly because they had had rather too little' (*KB* 111).

The Knox Brothers, like *Edward Burne-Jones*, exemplifies much that is characteristic in Fitzgerald's fiction. Habits of mind abundantly evident in the portraits of her father and three brothers include: the Edwardian fondness for understatement; extreme modesty and selflessness, tipping into melancholia; love of wit, puzzles, word games and absurdity, while thinking, at the same time, through the deepest questions of existence. As Hermione Lee observes, through growing up in a family containing every kind of religious adherence, from Evangelicals to Roman Catholics, from Anglicans to atheists, Fitzgerald came to the view that while religious divisions were futile, questions of belief and unbelief were nonetheless of vital concern (*PF* 3–8). In *The Knox Brothers*, this fascination with the inner life is handled with restraint, yet it underwrites the most poignant moments of characterization: 'In extreme illness, Wilfred had written...that we should be wrong to think of eternity as static, and, in consequence, boring. Why should we not go on, through all eternity, growing in love and in our power to love?' (*KB* 262). The biography records the brothers' lack of interest in pleasure or power, their eccentricity and integrity, their desire to serve, to be useful, and their need for affection above all. Fitzgerald's feeling for the less fortunate derives in part from the same concern in her father, in Wilfred and in Ronnie, but her interest in beauty allied to the useful came not from her father or uncles, but from Ruskin, Morris and Burne-Jones.

The style of *The Knox Brothers*, not quite as crammed with names, dates and places as *Edward Burne-Jones*, is vividly novelistic. Dialogue and reported speech bring the brothers to life, and distancing effects, such as an omniscient narrative standpoint, lends Fitzgerald's descriptions an air of authority and plausibility delightfully at odds with the absurdity of the behaviour described. In both world wars Dilly worked tirelessly as a cryptographer (most famously on efforts to break the Enigma machine used by the Germans),[9] and the pressure and intensity of the effort were reflected in his habits: 'His work was presented, as it had been in his Eton days, in inky scribbles on sheets of dirty paper, frequently mislaid. It was supposed that he kept his spectacles in his tobacco pouch to remind himself that he had taken the tobacco out of the spectacle case, substituting a piece of stale bread to remind himself that he was always hungry' (*KB* 127). The emotional life of these fiercely private men is deduced from their actions rather than their words. Ronnie's innocent encounter, when an Oxford undergraduate, with the daughters of a rural vicar prompts Fitzgerald to see in the memory a pivotal point in her uncle's life: 'it shows Ronnie delicately poised, in spite of all his achievements, between this way and that'. This point of suspension, alluded to so discreetly by Fitzgerald, contains all of life, mind, body and soul. Yet it is both a part of her discretion, and of her fascination with how to live in the world, that she immediately follows this insight into Ronnie's character with a broader philosophical observation and question: 'God speaks to us through the intellect, and through the intellect we should direct our lives. But if we are creatures of reason, what are we to do with our hearts?' (*KB* 78). Fitzgerald's personality and her own experiences are close to the surface in such moments. Conveyed in understated asides, such hints reveal to the careful reader something of the difficulties Fitzgerald had experienced in her own life: 'Occasionally they [the children] would write down a list of all the things they wanted but couldn't afford, and then burn the piece of paper. This is a device which is always worth trying' (*KB* 103).

The stylistic watchword in *The Knox Brothers* is distillation: of experience and of words themselves. Learning is always worn lightly, heightening pathos. After Wilfred's death in 1959, Eddie was invited by the University of Cambridge to speak about his brother in a lecture. Eddie, Fitzgerald reports, 'found that he could not do it. "Mortal things touch the mind," but even Virgil had not been able to explain them any farther than that' (*KB* 264). The quotation translates Aeneas's lament, 'mentem mortalia tangunt' (*Aeneid* 1.462), upon recalling the destruction of his family and home. The strength of Eddie's feelings was such that he was unable to explain or put them into words, something even Virgil's epic poem about loss, exile and fate had not managed to do. Such unobtrusive use of quotation to convey, and in a subtle way, exalt deeply held feeling is one of the most poignant yet least remarked features of Fitzgerald's writing.

The method and manner of Fitzgerald's writing in *The Knox Brothers* clearly owe a debt to the stylistic traits of her chief biographical sources: her grandfather E. A. Knox's *Reminiscences of an Octogenarian* (1934), her aunt Winifred Peck's *A Little Learning* (1952) and *Home for the Holidays* (1955), and Evelyn Waugh's *The Life of Ronald Knox* (1959). Fitzgerald draws heavily upon these sources (quotation marks signalling her debt), often sticking close to their wording. But as she did later with the sources for her historical novels (such as her use of Baedeker for *The Beginning of Spring*), she added details and remoulded prose rhythms to intensify both pathos and comedy. A good example of Fitzgerald's reworking of sources is her telling of the early encounter of the brothers, in their schoolroom, with their stepmother, Ethel Knox (née Newton). The source for Fitzgerald's account was a *Daily Chronicle* article by Mrs Knox herself (quoted verbatim in Waugh's *Ronald Knox*), which reads as follows:

> Eddie Knox occupied the single shabby armchair, reading aloud with ribald comments Smiles's *Self Help*. Dillwyn sat lost in a Greek lexicon, Wilfred manipulated a toy train, the girls played a duet on the piano, Ronald lay before the fire with Wood's *Natural History*. They greeted her [Ethel Newton] politely and continued with their pleasures. She withdrew and said to the Bishop: 'They really are clever children. They can occupy themselves.'
>
> Five minutes later the scared face of Winifred appeared at the

study door. 'You must come up. The boys are murdering one another.'

She found the little boys cowering in corners; the furniture was overturned; *Self Help* had gone out of the window, and Eddie and Dillwyn were locked in what seemed a death grapple.[10]

Fitzgerald renders the scene as follows:

> Mrs. K would look into the schoolroom and note that all was well, the girls banging out a duet on the piano, the little boys quietly playing, Eddie and Dilly sarcastically reading to each other out of Smiles's *Self-Help*, then be summoned urgently a few minutes later to find *Self-Help* sailing out of the window, Eddie and Dilly locked in a death grapple, Wilfred and Ronnie cowering in corners with their hands folded over their bellies to protect their most valuable possession, their wind. (KB 34)

Numerous small differences distinguish Fitzgerald's from Mrs Knox's account. In Fitzgerald's retelling, the whole scene is compressed into one fluid sentence, dynamic and absurd, more consistently past continuous than the original, with details of the children's individual activities reduced to the minimum, and the death grapple placed in the penultimate rather than punchline position. This, in Fitzgerald's version, is reserved for the cowering younger brothers, who are pictured protecting 'their most valuable possession, their wind'. This is an unexpected, yet characteristically Rabelaisian turn by Fitzgerald; we expect a reference to genitals but get wind (or breath), an Old English monosyllable rather than a Latinate trisyllable. Wind, in its terminal position in the scene, makes the reader laugh (at the word's sound and connotations) and think, hinting simultaneously as it does at the boys' bodily and spiritual (airy) selves. Such are the small but significant ways in which Fitzgerald recast her sources.

The Knox Brothers contains in early forms many of the elements found in Fitzgerald's novels: from detective fiction and delight in solving problems (*The Golden Child*), to Ronnie's motto, 'Do the difficult thing' (*The Bookshop*), and to wit, emotional restraint, the unsaid, and the eternal questions of why we are here and how we should live. Dilly's Edwardian Cambridge, with its panoply of eccentric college societies, including one known as the 'As It Were In Contradistinction

Society' (*KB* 60), provides the setting for *Gate of Angels*, and the model for The Disobligers' Society at which Fred Fairly has to oppose the motion: 'That the soul does not exist, has never existed, and that it is not desirable that it should exist' (*GA* 52). The vivid accounts of the brothers' rectory childhoods foreshadow the families and households Fitzgerald creates especially with fiction such as the Gentilinis in *Innocence*, the Reids in *The Beginning of Spring*, the Fairlys in *Gate of Angels*, and the Hardenbergs in *The Blue Flower*. Yet such family groups, as Fitzgerald knew, are always subject to change. Even in the midst of the Knox brothers' schooldays, living and studying together in St Philip's Rectory in Birmingham, 'there were stirrings, intimations of nature and poetry and human weakness', which could never be confided to their father, the bishop, or to their stepmother, Mrs K. 'There were certain aspects of sea and cloud and open country that brought to them, as it did to Housman's Shropshire Lad, "into my heart an air that kills"'. Cory's epitaph, beginning, 'They told me, Heraclitus, they told me you were dead, / They brought me bitter news to hear, and bitter tears to shed', had the power, over four lifetimes, 'beyond "rational argument"', 'to remind them of each other, across time and space' (*KB* 41). The same keen sorrow, of love's heroic futility in the face of time and fate, makes the ending of *The Blue Flower*, and indeed the ending of all novels, as Frank Kermode proposed in his *Sense of an Ending*, almost unendurable. Fitzgerald herself admitted that there were certain less attractive things that she had been unable to say about the brothers – about their explosive temper, depression, aloofness, and sexuality – not only because she couldn't bring herself to speak of them and chose to present a romanticized view, but because she wished not to hurt anyone's feelings.[11] In this regard Fitzgerald was merely sticking to her principle that biographers should feel warmly towards their subjects. As she wrote to her friend, the novelist Francis King: 'I expect my uncles were dislikeable, but I loved them and got used to them.'[12]

CHARLOTTE MEW AND HER FRIENDS (1984)

Published between *At Freddie's* (1982) and *Innocence* (1986), Fitzgerald's life of the little-known English poet Charlotte Mew marks the division between her early and late work. Certainly, *Charlotte Mew* is the most purely novelistic of Fitzgerald's three biographies. Mew (1869–1928) wrote poetry, stories, essays and a play; her work was published in the journals of the day and in two books of verse, *The Farmer's Bride* (1915) and *The Rambling Sailor* (1929). Though read today chiefly by specialists, Mew's strikingly original poetry was admired by her contemporaries, including Thomas Hardy, John Masefield, Siegfried Sassoon, Virginia Woolf and Walter de la Mare. Mew's was often an agonized life: haunted by a family history of mental illness, though she herself never quite succumbed, living for many years in straitened circumstances and falling unhappily in love, at least twice, with women who rejected her advances. In 1928, aged forty-nine, despondent at the death of her beloved sister Anne, Mew committed suicide by drinking a bottle of disinfectant. 'During this time Charlotte apparently lost some battle, or perhaps, as she had suggested at the end of *The Quiet House*, she had gone to meet herself at last' (*CM* 225).

Fitzgerald's attraction to Mew had a personal dimension. Her father, E. V. Knox, had been asked by *Punch* to parody well-known poets of the day, including Mew (*CM* 187). Fitzgerald herself remembered being taken as a little girl to the Poetry Bookshop in Devonshire Street, run by Harold and Alida Monro, where Mew gave her first public poetry readings: 'this was a time when writing and reading poetry was a natural activity'.[13] Fitzgerald saw Mew as someone, alongside poets such as A. E. Housman and Rupert Brooke, who contributed to 'the last body of English poetry to be actually read by ordinary people, for pleasure' (*CM* 150) – a view Fitzgerald had held from her earliest days.[14] Fitzgerald was also drawn to the tragic course of Mew's life. 'After a brilliant start, she knew she had failed to meet her friends' expectations' (*CM* 99). It is Mew, as much as any character in Fitzgerald's fiction, who fits the description of one born to be defeated: 'She was marked out to lose, with too much courage ever to accept it' (*CM* 30).[15]

Fitzgerald's fine-grained characterization of Mew is reflected in the book's index. Under 'personality' come seventeen different subheadings: 'depressions', 'divided self', 'excitable, passionate', 'fascinating, entertaining', 'fierce and shy with strangers', 'haunted by recurrent images', 'indifference (apparent)', 'interest in prostitutes', 'like a boy', 'as "Miss Lotti"', 'love or longing for' (a subset including: 'children', 'Christmas', 'cigarettes', 'fisherman's life', 'friends', 'France', 'London and Londoners', 'Nature', 'sea', 'thought of death', 'trees'), 'lover of women', 'practical side', 'religious experience', 'sense of guilt', 'small size', 'taste in clothes' (CM 298–9). Fitzgerald's portrait of Mew dwells on the child Charlotte's sense of guilt, of being watched, of 'a day of eyes', inherited in part from her nurse, the nonconformist Elizabeth Goodman:

> ' "A day of eyes", of transcendental vision, when the very roses . . . challenge the pureness of our gaze, and the grass marks the manner of our going, and the sky hangs like a gigantic curtain, veiling the grace which, watching us invisibly, we somehow fail to see. It judged in those days my scamped and ill-done tasks. It viewed my childish cruelties and still, with wider range, it views and judges them now.' From the age of six or seven Lotti, 'full of the joy of life', knew that she was guilty. (CM 16)

Alida Monro, in her first-hand account of Mew, wrote that 'She was very much two people, though she was unaware of it',[16] and Fitzgerald develops and reiterates this idea throughout her biography. 'She was determined to remain Miss Lotti – a lady, even if she made rather an odd one. There is pathos in this clinging to gentility by a free spirit, who seemed born to have nothing to do with it' (CM 45).

As in her creation of fictional characters, Fitzgerald enriches her portrait of Mew by vividly evoking the people, places and times she knew. Of Mew's mother, Anna Maria, Fitzgerald observes, 'What is certain is that she was a tiny, pretty, silly young woman who grew, in time, to be a very silly old one' (CM 6). Of Henry Harland, the publisher of *The Yellow Book*, Fitzgerald affectionately remarks: 'the dying Harland was Harland still. Asked by the lady next to him to pass the salt, he exclaimed: "Dear lady, it is yours! And may I not also pass you the mustard?"' (CM 60). The Poetry Bookshop, where Mew first read her poetry in public, holds a special place in the narrative. It is a meeting place for the poets of the day – including Wilfred Owen, a visiting Robert Frost, and Wilfred Gibson, who 'lived in a kind of cupboard, marked "in case of fire, access to the roof is through this room"' (*CM* 147) and was a stage for Mew's muted entrance into the world of poetry: 'At about five minutes to six the swing door opened and out of the autumn fog came a tiny figure, apparently a maiden aunt, dressed in a hard felt hat and a small-sized man's overcoat. She was asked, "Are you Charlotte Mew?" and replied, with a slight smile, "I am sorry to say I am."' (*CM* 154)

Fitzgerald draws closely on Alida Monro's memoir here, and elsewhere on Joy Grant's history of the Poetry Bookshop, in each case adding small details (such as the 'hard felt hat') to enhance the scene, and altering sentence length, punctuation and phrasing to increase the drama.[17] Distilling her own research, Fitzgerald places Mew in the midst of an entire epoch, helping the reader to understand Charlotte's individual response to the world around her:

> It was a cautious start into the new century, from which so much was expected.... For everyone who could afford them, there were hopes. From the anxious edge of the professional and artistic world Charlotte got her view of the gospels of Life and Joy, the new call to the open road ('going I know not where'), the commitment to self-purification and vegetarian diets, to the City Beautiful and to youth, energy, humanity and fresh air.... Charlotte, just turned thirty, tried to prepare herself to be carried forward or if necessary, to be left behind. Her face at this time took on its habitual curious expression, with her strong eyebrows raised in a perpetual half-moon, as though she had just heard a joke, or perhaps thought that if life is a joke it is not a very good one. (*CM* 71)

Fitzgerald had written often about poetry for *Punch* and *World Review*. She does so in *Charlotte Mew* with a keen appreciation both of the motives for poetry and of poetic technique. Speaking of Mew's art of impersonation, Fitzgerald asks 'why do poets impersonate at all? They may do it because they have a great deal to hide, or because (like Browning) they haven't quite enough. They may (like Byron) be too energetic or too self-indulgent to contain themselves, they may (like Eliot) want to escape from emotion, or (like Yeats) from the unsatisfactory limitation of self. To Charlotte Mew impersonation was necessary, rather than helpful. "The quality of emotion," she thought, was "the first requirement of poetry... for good work one must accept the discipline that can be got, while the emotion is given to one." And what she needed to give a voice to, as she also explained, was the *cri de coeur* – that is, the moment when the emotion unmistakeably concentrates itself into a few words' (CM 106). The *cri de coeur* is unmissable in Mew's poems, frequently given discomforting form in 'free rhyming verse, following line by line the impulses of the speaker, like jets of blood from a wound' (CM 124–5). As in her critical writing, Fitzgerald's command of the literary context is assured but lightly worn. Speaking about the 'thirty-bob-a-weeker', who is the subject of 'In Nunhead Cemetery': 'He had been the hero (if he can ever be called that) of Ella's *Irremediable*, but he is also Kipling's young chemist's assistant possessed by the spirit of John Keats, and Forster's Leonard Bast, struggling to educate himself, and the "pale bespectacled face" Edward Thomas described at the office window. Very few of these dreamers, beyond Wells's Kipps, ever get free from the desk and the counter, to finish up alive with the right woman. To aim too high seems to be destructive in itself' (*CM* 73). The breadth of reference here is impressive but never gratuitous: each literary parallel freshly shades for us the figure in Mew's poem.

The connection between the vividly episodic *Charlotte Mew*, all extraneous information pared away, and Fitzgerald's oblique, elliptical later novels, especially *The Blue Flower*, is striking. There is a parallel too between Mew's art of impersonation and Fitzgerald's in those later works, going beyond straightforward representation to inhabit the voices and fragmentary consciousnesses of characters such as Chiara Ridolfi, Frank Reid, Daisy Saunders and Friedrich von Hardenberg. And it is in these late novels too, more than anywhere else in Fitzgerald's writing, that the everyday world shines most often with that strange radiance glimpsed, almost unbearably, by Charlotte Mew:

>   Here, even, in this corner where my little candle shines
>   And overhead the lancet-window glows
>   With golds and crimsons you could almost drink
> To know how jewels taste

('Madeleine in Church'; *CM* 248)

3

Early Novels

Between 1977 and 1982 Penelope Fitzgerald, then in her early sixties, published five short novels in a remarkable surge of creativity: *The Golden Child*, *The Bookshop*, *Offshore*, *Human Voices* and *At Freddie's*.[1] Throughout these years she continued to teach at the sixth-form crammer Westminster Tutors, only finally giving it up in 1987, aged seventy. Each of these 'early' novels draws upon Fitzgerald's own life, and all but one contain female protagonists who resemble Fitzgerald herself either in her youth or middle-age. ('Early' here refers specifically to Fitzgerald's career as a novelist; she had, as the preceding chapters of this book make clear, been writing for decades before her first novel was published.) In her later years Fitzgerald sometimes downplayed her first five novels: *The Golden Child* 'was only a joke, such as I used to make then'; *The Bookshop* 'will seem very old-fashioned by now'; and *Human Voices* she 'couldn't quite get... to hang together, but it was the best I could do' (*SI* 430, 203, 381). Critical responses too have been mixed. While both *The Bookshop* and *Offshore* were shortlisted for the Booker Prize, the highest critical praise is almost always reserved for Fitzgerald's later historical novels. This has an unfortunate effect, making the earlier phase of Fitzgerald's novel-writing career look like a mere period of apprenticeship for the later.[2]

Thinking this way risks underrating the earlier works' particular pleasures. These include the deft evocation of wholly believable times and places, often on the periphery of things – a windswept outpost in Suffolk, the houseboat community on Battersea Reach, the raffish backstage world of *At Freddie's*; finely observed characters swept along, bravely, reluctantly, on cross-currents of thought, feeling and happenstance; sudden parabolic swerves in mood and story arising with a recognizable yet surprising logic from the situations in which people find themselves; dialogue that is by turns oblique, elliptical and heartbreakingly frank; submerged but telling allusions to other books, stories, plays and people; sharp criticism of cruelty in all its forms, and a corresponding sympathy for those who suffer from it. These five early novels may not be perfect – for A. N. Wilson, only one, *At Freddie's*, is 'pure gold' – but they all, without exception, cram more joyfully subversive wit, feeling and artistry within their narrow spans than do most novels of twice the length, and all richly repay re-reading.

THE GOLDEN CHILD (1977)

Fitzgerald dedicated her first novel, *The Golden Child*, to her husband Desmond. In interviews Fitzgerald always claimed that she had written the book to amuse him as he lay dying of cancer, but this was only part of her motivation. A second part was, 'I needed to make some money';[3] a third was 'largely to get rid of my annoyance: 1. about the Tutankhamen Exhib: as I'm certain everything in it was a forgery, and: 2. about someone who struck me as particularly unpleasant when I was obliged to go to a lot of museums &c. to find out about Burne-Jones' (*SI* 240). Indeed, part of *The Golden Child's* appeal lies in its keen satirical edge, voiced through the book's playful engagement with the conventions of the mystery genre. Yet despite containing many ingredients familiar from her better-known works, *The Golden Child* is the least satisfying of Fitzgerald's works. In part this was because the publisher insisted that Fitzgerald cut characters, sub-plots and scenes, and even the book's epilogue. But there are other, more intrinsic reasons why *The Golden Child* stands apart from Fitzgerald's other novels and short stories, as this section will show.

The story of *The Golden Child* can be told in a few sentences. A thinly disguised British Museum holds a hugely successful exhibition of golden artefacts from the African Garamantian civilization, including the mummified remains of the 'Golden Child'.[4] Crowds queue for hours in the bitter cold just to glimpse the precious relics. Gradually it becomes clear to a handful of staff that the objects in the exhibition are fake. The real golden artefacts are in fact secretly held in Moscow as collateral against a Russian loan to Garamantia. Farce and mayhem ensue. Murders, attempted murders, deceit and deception descend upon the usually imperturbable world of the Museum, and increasingly frantic efforts are made to keep the truth from the public.

The novel's setting and genre drew variously on Fitzgerald's life and interests. Fitzgerald attended the Tutankhamun exhibition of 1972, saw the crowds, and thought about the awful, delicious possibility of it all being bogus.[5] She may also have heard or read something similar about the British Museum's 'Treasures of Romania' exhibition, held just a year previously.[6] Waring Smith's bewildering visit to Russia to see Professor Semyonov, who turns out to be an invention of the Clown Splitov, draws upon Fitzgerald's notes and memories of her own two-week trip to Moscow and Leningrad in 1975 with her daughter Maria (*PF* 235). Some of the novel's territory she had visited before: encountering museum curators and art historians in her research for *Edward Burne-Jones*; unravelling detective stories, puzzles and cryptography in *The Knox Brothers*. Yet whatever the precise origin of the plot, Fitzgerald captures intimately and satirically the Museum's eccentric, class-bound inner workings, its infighting and labyrinthine premises – anticipating in a dark vein her later treatment of the BBC in *Human Voices*.

More than in any other of Fitzgerald's novels, the characters in *The Golden Child* sharply divide into heroes and villains. The greatest sympathy is reserved for Waring Smith, a junior Exhibition officer, who is 'young, normal, unimpressed, sincere and worried'. As a married man Smith worries chiefly about his mortgage, the 'sum of £118 a month' payable to the Whitstable and Protective Building Society. Yet crucially, foreshadowing the equally harassed young married couple in *Innocence* or the von Rockenthiens in *The Blue Flower*, Waring Smith 'had an instinct for happiness against which even the Whitstable and Protective Society could not prevail' (*GC* 28, 30). Possession of this instinct always qualifies a character in Fitzgerald's fiction for approval, or at least understanding. Other qualities also rate highly: honesty, sincerity, compassion, emotion, sensuality, eccentricity and suffering. Among the novel's principal heroes, Sir William Simpkin is authentic, manly, penetrating and kind, while Professor Untermensch, obsessive, enthusiastic, more practical and worldly than he looks, is an underdog, a lover of knowledge for its own sake. Len Coker, in Conservation and Technical Services, imagines ancient Garamantia as an ideal society, like William Morris's in *News from Nowhere*: he is roughly affectionate, trenchantly opposed to privilege, yet morally flexible. Speaking of his relationship with Sir William's secretary, Dousha, he admits: 'I'm lucky. Not environmentally, not socio-economically, but from a sex-angle, I'm lucky. I'm well aware that we're very different types, but egalitarianism doesn't mean that all partners must be similar. That's another bourgeois delusion' (*GC* 197–8).

The villains are equally clearly delineated. Besetting sins include unprincipled ambition, snobbery, superficial expertise, social smoothness, fakery and deceit. Chief among the rogues are Sir John Allison, Museum Director, suave and ruthless (based on Kenneth Clark, broadcaster and former Director of the National Gallery), and Marcus Hawthorne-Mannering, Keeper of Funerary Art, 'exceedingly thin...with movements full of graceful suffering...he was deeply pained by almost everything he saw about him' (*GC* 18). Hawthorne-Mannering is mocked for his preciousness (his unflattering nickname is the May Queen). This is the closest Fitzgerald comes in her work to homophobia, but her point is that Hawthorne-Mannering's fine feeling and recoil from normal human life is a failing of simple humanity rather than one associated with sexuality or sexual preference. Tite-Live Rochegrosse-Bergson, a spoof amalgam of the French thinkers Roland Barthes, Jacques Derrida and Claude Lévi-Strauss, turns out to have been guilty of looting art treasures under the Vichy Government (*GC* 243). Fitzgerald's satire is a wickedly pointed attack on the fashion in cultural studies of the early- and mid-1970s for French philosophies, structuralism and deconstruction.[7] Yet Fitzgerald's antipathy to what she felt was an abstract, over-ingenious branch of higher nonsense was not merely a product of her frustration as a teacher of English in the 1960s and 70s, but reached back to her earliest book reviews for *Punch*. As early as 1947, for instance, she had observed of G. Wilson Knight's *The Crown of Life*:

'Prospero is compared to Nietzsche and to the Chinese saint Tripitaka...Professor Knight strikes out so many brilliant notions that the reader feels almost guilty when he finds he is not convinced.'[8] Or even earlier, in 1943, of a study of Dante: 'It should be mentioned that Mr. Williams's style is so careful, so delicate...that it is hard at times to discover what on earth (or heaven, or hell) he is driving at.'[9]

If characterization in *The Golden Child* leans towards caricature, the core constituents of Fitzgerald's writing style are still clearly in evidence. Professor Untermensch is the vehicle for Fitzgerald's mordant wit and logic: 'The Garamantians had no conception of the present. They thought only of the past and the future; hence, they were happy' (*GC* 194). Fluid narration, slipping from the third person to free indirect speech, is also present as Waring Smith seeks out Len Coker at his flat and suddenly the reader finds him or herself seeing things directly from Smith's perspective: 'the unhopeful Greek proprietor indicated with a nod that you could walk straight through, move a pile of crates aside, and go up the dark staircase to Mr Coker's place' (*GC* 183).

Literary allusion, too, as in Fitzgerald's other novels, is deftly worked in, enriching the story's texture, depth and mystery. Following a meeting between Sir John and Hawthorne-Mannering: 'The Director made a note in his private diary. "H-M perhaps a good deal stronger character than he looks. The only emperor is the emperor of ice-cream"' (*GC* 92). The allusion is to the Wallace Stevens poem of the same title, which gestures enigmatically at the brute fact that life goes on even in the face of death, and that those who survive and prosper are the most animal and instinctive among us.[10] The quotation reveals both Allison's view of Hawthorne-Mannering and his own inclination to the reticence, riddles, yet lyricism of Stevens. Other allusions establish literary associations between characters in different ways. The home address of Tite-Live Rochegrosse-Bergson in Paris, rue Baron de Charlus (*GC* 214), associates the fraudulent literary theorist with the homosexual nobleman in Proust's *À la recherche du temps perdu*. Waring shows his love for Sir William by quoting Byron to Inspector Mace, about Sir William's care for his pipes: 'Dear is the helpless creature we defend' (*Don Juan*, Canto 1) (*GC* 221). Waring's literary romanticism is revealed in the canto's conclusion, unvoiced in the novel, that sweeter still than such defence is 'first and passionate love'. Fitzgerald, as always in her fiction, only has her characters recall lines that *they* would have known, but the few words are well spent. Brief snatches of quotation endow previously unremarkable characters with new layers of temperament, feeling and individuality.

As topical as the museum setting of *The Golden Child* was, the novel's literary origins lay further back. Anticipating by a quarter of a century her invention of Garamantia, Fitzgerald's Tisshara stories in *World Review* create: 'another purely fictive nation (complete with folklore, relics, dolls, and pictographs) used to parody and mock the contemporary world'.[11] Fitzgerald herself acknowledged that she set out to write a mystery novel according to the kind of rules formulated by her uncle Ronald Knox in detective stories such as *The Viaduct Murder* (1925) and *The Body in the Silo* (1933): 'mystery stories should have clues, false clues, suspects and a complete explanation in the last chapter'.[12] The more diffuse influence of Conan Doyle's Sherlock Holmes is also in evidence, though fused with a comic element close to farce, a characteristic feature of all of her novels. As Fitzgerald explained: 'True farce is not, as is so often said, based on the *improbable*, but is the *logical result of pursuing probable desires to the bitter end*'.[13] This logic holds true for *The Golden Child*, but the cuts Fitzgerald was persuaded to make by Colin Haycraft her editor at Duckworth including a series of high-level Cabinet meetings, a subplot about the affections of Sir John's daughter for the son of Waring Smith's immediate supervisor, and happy endings for each of the characters, distort the clear working out of the story, and, in turn, the comedy and its pathos. Were the cancelled chapters and passages to be restored Fitzgerald's achievement could be gauged more fairly.[14]

Even restored to full-length, however, *The Golden Child* still may not please as Fitzgerald's other novels do. The characterization of Waring Smith, and his troubled relationship with his wife Haggie, interests readers but doesn't make an irresistible claim on their sympathy. Nor, despite the murders, attempted murders and fraud on a massive scale, is the sense of threat sufficiently sinister or real. The surface wit is just a fraction too polished and taut to allow any stronger emotions than pleasurable indignation and mock horror at the venial doings of the craven and power-hungry. Yet to say that *The Golden Child* is the least of Fitzgerald's novels is hardly a criticism. The book still contains in abundance the compelling attraction of Fitzgerald's acute intelligence, her way of looking at the world, verging on prescience, that seems so often to anticipate and articulate our own – just with more precision and art. Two unfinished novels by Fitzgerald from the late 1970s, *The Iron Bridge*, featuring Professor Untermensch, and *Sale or Return*, inspired by the 1977 auction at Sotheby's of Lord Rosebery's treasures at Mentmore Towers, promised more in the vein of *The Golden Child*, reflecting Fitzgerald's enthusiasm for the mystery genre (*PF* 252). Both projects, however, were eventually put aside as Fitzgerald set out to write a very different kind of novel, *The Bookshop*.

THE BOOKSHOP (1978)

For the setting, characters and events of *The Bookshop*, Fitzgerald again drew on her own life. In an interview Fitzgerald explained that after finishing *The Golden Child* she hadn't been able to think of any more mystery stories and for this reason had chosen to write 'a straight novel about a bookshop I worked in...which had a real poltergeist'.[15] In 1957 Fitzgerald had moved out of London with her three young children to Southwold in East Suffolk, living there for the next four years and working part-time in the Sole Bay Bookshop, run by Phyllis Neame, to whom the book is dedicated ('an old friend'). *The Bookshop*, written two decades later, recaptures in evocative detail the provincial social world of the seaside town at the end of the 1950s, exploring the highs and lows of human character. As Fitzgerald came to see it, 'The novel is really the report of a battle, a very minor engagement, of course, but important to the wounded'.[16] That the wounds ran deep is evident from the sharpness of some of the characterization, although Mrs Neame, having read the book, said that everyone was a lot nicer in real life.[17] The disparity between Phyllis Neame's benign view of life in Southwold and Fitzgerald's portrayal of lines drawn in *The Bookshop* can be attributed, in part, to imaginative licence. But it is also important to remember that Fitzgerald wrote *The Bookshop* soon after the death of her husband Desmond. It is hard not to think that at least some of the book's sense of defeat derived from this more recent experience of loss.

The novel's plot is simplicity itself. Florence Green, a widow in middle age, decides to open a bookshop in the Suffolk town of Hardborough. She decides this in part because she 'had recently come to wonder whether she hadn't a duty to make it clear to herself, and possibly to others, that she existed in her own right' (*BK* 2). A suitable property has to be found – The Old House and oyster warehouse – and a loan with the bank negotiated. Florence successfully overcomes these initial obstacles and sets up in business. Some in the town provide practical help. The Sea Scouts, under the direction of Mr Raven the marshman, paint and put up shelves; ten-year-old Christine Gipping assists in the shop itself; and customers come to buy the books, cards and calendars or subscribe to the circulating library. Florence even has a conspicuous success when she decides to stock Nabokov's *Lolita*. But this is the beginning of her downfall: 'All the tradespeople were now either slightly or emphatically hostile to the Old House Bookshop. It was decided not to ask her to join the Inner Wheel of the Hardborough and District Rotary Club' (*BK* 109). Added to which, the snobbish, well-connected Mrs Violet Gamart covets the Old House, wishing to set up an Arts Centre in Hardborough to rival the successful arts scene in neighbouring Aldeburgh. At the same time, a poltergeist, or 'rapper' as the locals call it, haunts the Old House, banging doors, rattling windows and sending temperatures plummeting. Despite the support of a few loyal friends, including the reclusive Mr Brundish, Florence is forced to give up the lease on the property and sell off her stock to settle debts. The ending is as heartbreaking and pessimistic as any in Fitzgerald's writing: 'At Flintmarket she took the 10.46 to Liverpool Street. As the train drew out of the station she sat with the head bowed in shame, because the town in which she had lived for nearly ten years had not wanted a bookshop' (*BK* 156).

Florence's decision to stock *Lolita* places the events of the novel at a turning point in British social history, when the permissiveness of the 1960s took over from the buttoned-down post-war 1950s. Everything is treated realistically: Hardborough is Southwold, the Laze is the Blyth, Saxford is Blythburgh. The supernatural too is viewed as a fact of life. Phyllis Neame recalled that 'all old hands in Southwold know of this poltergeist which is supposed to roam up & down the High Street'.[18] We, the readers, take the rapper seriously because Florence, Christine and others in the novel do, reflecting Fitzgerald's sense that some things which are inexplicable must simply be accepted rather than understood. Yet the novel's tragicomic world is, as Fitzgerald intended it to be, a heightened version of reality, the tensely dramatic playing out of a battle, albeit 'a very minor engagement'. The small town contains every species of villainy: the mendacity and egoism of Violet Gamart; the laziness and selfishness of Milo North, who works for the BBC in some unspecified capacity; the condescension, inflexibility and spinelessness of local lawyers and bank managers; and the apologetic passivity before Mrs Gamart's will of her friends and even her husband, the General. Fitzgerald's personal struggles provide the emotional substrate of the novel. Her principles, alluded to in the two books Florence takes with her when she leaves – Ruskin's *Unto This Last*, which honours the dignity of labour, and Bunyan's spiritual autobiography, *Grace Abounding*, which gives voice to the oppressed – form the book's larger moral argument and give it bite: 'She blinded herself... by pretending for a while that human beings are not divided into exterminators and exterminatees, with the former, at any given moment, predominating' (*BK* 37). But it is literature itself, and Fitzgerald's pleasure in its inner workings, that transform these thoughts and feelings into art. 'Balzac', Fitzgerald wrote, 'was the presiding genius of this little book' (*SI* 504), referring to Balzac's novella of petty provincial conflicts, *Le Curé de Tours* (1832), and to the echo in Violet Gamart's surname of Balzac's wicked Mademoiselle Sophie Gamard.

Two kinds of scene in *The Bookshop* are most vivid. The first is the arresting image, declaring its farcical oddity and that of the world: the heron awkwardly trying in mid-flight to swallow an eel; Florence hauling on the tongue of an old Suffolk Punch, while the marshman Mr Raven files its yellow teeth; both images comparable in their mute emblematic significance to the cows wallowing among the willows at the beginning of *The Gate of Angels*, or the moment in *The Blue Flower* when Fritz holds a severed finger and signet ring in his mouth. The second kind of scene is the dramatic encounter or set-piece, crucial stages in the conflict, such as Mrs Gamart's party, her visit to the bookshop (when Christine raps her over the knuckles with a ruler), Florence taking tea with Mr Brundish, or Mr Brundish's climactic head-to-head with Mrs Gamart. The fascination of such scenes lies in their unpredictability – the painful irony of the missed opportunity, the sudden outburst of intense emotion long kept down, the silent pathos of the unsaid. In the account of Florence's visit to Mr Brundish, after several pages of talk:

> a different element entered the conversation, as perceptible as a shift in the wind. Mr Brundish made no attempt to check this, on the contrary he seemed to be relieved that some prearranged point had been reached....
> 'Let me tell you what I admire in human beings. I value most the one virtue which they share with gods and animals, and which need not therefore be referred to as a virtue. I refer to courage. You, Mrs Green, possess that quality in abundance.'
> She knew perfectly well, sitting in the dull afternoon light, with the ludicrous array of slop basins and tureens in front of her, that loneliness was speaking to loneliness, and that he was appealing to her directly. The words had come out slowly, as though between each one she was being given the opportunity of a response. But while the moment hung in the balance and she struggled to put some kind of order into what she felt or half guessed, Mr Brundish sighed deeply. Perhaps he found her wanting in some respect. His direct gaze turned gradually away from her, and he looked down at his plate. The necessity to make conversation returned.
> 'This cake would have been poison to my sister,' he observed. (*BK* 103)

The situation of this passage, of 'loneliness...speaking to loneliness', is territory familiar from Barbara Pym, in novels such as *Autumn Quartet*. But the treatment of it is Fitzgerald's own. The writing sticks close to Florence's thoughts yet remains in the third person. We follow her confusion but are given room to wonder, without being told, what it was that 'she felt or half guessed'. The rhythm of the prose is unpredictable. Long, multi-clausal sentences build emotional suspense before shortening again as the moment passes. We sense, with regret, that an opportunity has been missed. On other occasions Fitzgerald's narration slips into free indirect speech, signalled by dashes:

The suspicion that she [Florence] was clinging on simply because her vanity had been wounded was unbearable. – Of course, Mrs Gamart, whom I shall never speak of or refer to as Violet, it was Milo North you had in mind. Install him immediately. My little book business can be fitted in anywhere. I only ask you not to allow the conventions to be defied too rapidly – East Suffolk isn't used to it. Kattie will have to live, for the first few years at least, in the oyster warehouse. (*BK* 36)

The switch to internal monologue intensifies the abjectness of Florence's humiliation. The barbed sarcasm brings us uncomfortably close to the rawness of her feelings. She had foolishly allowed herself to dream. Now she must be punished.

Fitzgerald's relish for and finely judged handling of physical and verbal details enhances both plausibility and comedy. Suffolk diction flavours the speech of Wally: 'He's trying to reverse round in one go, do he'll go straight through your backhouse' (*BK* 55); Christine: 'I'll fare to do that after tea, when I'm at home' (*BK* 63); and her mother, Mrs Gipping, referring to the rapper: 'That knows not to waste its time, I dare say' (*BK* 126). Regional proverbs evoke the character of the place: 'in a hard blow the little brick-and-tile houses seemed to cling to each other, as the saying went, like a sailor's child' (*BK* 37). The local perspective, comically parochial, is always kept in mind: 'Handel's *Messiah* is sung every Christmas, you know, both in Norwich and at the Albert Hall, in London' (*BK* 52). Rhythms of dialogue follow patterns of speech: '"Don't you worry about the black edges," Raven said. "He had those envelopes done it must have been in 1919, when they all came back from the first war, and I was still a nipper, and Mrs Brundish died"' (*BK* 47). Children, especially Christine, are never anything less than forthright: '"I like this old tray," she said. "You can put that down for me in your will"' (*BK* 77). In narration too Fitzgerald subtly conveys a character's way of speaking: 'even the dejected-looking Mrs Deben ... knew where Florence was going to tea on the Sunday' (*BK* 96). Blink and you miss it – Fitzgerald's narrator would never say 'on the Sunday' (she would say 'on Sunday'), but Mrs Deben, the fishmonger's wife, would. This, then, is Mrs Deben's thought, *her* definite article. The effect is to lift Mrs Deben off the page and into life, to make us believe implicitly in the reality of even such a minor character.

Many of the first reviews of *The Bookshop* were belittling, relegating it to the 'school of anguished women's fiction'.[19] Some readers, though, were more perceptive and to the surprise of many critics and of Fitzgerald herself the book was shortlisted for the Booker Prize. The reasons are not hard to see. Fitzgerald's patterning rather than plotting (to adopt a distinction made by Edmund Gordon) of her story of tragicomic failure and the book's constant subversion of expectation declare its originality, albeit in an understated way.[20] Examples of Fitzgerald's trademark off-kilter, almost Wildean, epigrams abound. Mr Brundish, approving Florence's proposal to sell *Lolita* to the inhabitants of Hardborough, observes: 'They won't understand it, but that is all to the good. Understanding makes the mind lazy' (*BK* 101). This expresses perfectly Fitzgerald's own sense of what a novel should do. Keep the reader awake, don't explain too much, not everything can or should be understood at first glance. With time readers and critics have also come to see how, unlike Balzac in *Le Curé de Tours*, or Jane Austen, or other novelists famous for painting on a small canvas, Fitzgerald's witty dissection of small-town manners and feuds extends far beyond the social world 'into a different, larger atmosphere', as in this passing remark on late middle-age, upper middle-class East Suffolk water-colourists:

> All their pictures looked much the same. Framed, they hung in sitting-rooms, while outside the windows the empty, washed-out, unarranged landscape stretched away to the transparent sky. (*BK* 68)[21]

In such hints at something larger, 'stretching away to the transparent sky', *The Bookshop* is entirely characteristic of Fitzgerald's writing. Like all of her autobiographical novels (and unlike her later, historical fictions, most of which end by looking forwards), *The Bookshop* records a completed episode or chapter in a character's life. Told in retrospect, these chapters are all the more poignant for their unrecoverable distance from the present, like things we should have said when we still had the chance.

OFFSHORE (1979)

Offshore, like all of Fitzgerald's early novels, turns life into fiction. In 1960 the Fitzgeralds had moved back to London from Southwold to live on *Grace*, a battered Thames sailing barge on Battersea Reach. Everything was a struggle: there were constant money worries, Fitzgerald was exhausted from teaching (first at the Italia Conti stage school, and then at Queen's Gate School and Westminster Tutors), and her relationship with Desmond, who was often the worse for drink, was at a low ebb (*PF* 141–7). The central character in *Offshore*, a young Canadian woman, Nenna James, is as surely imbued – as is Florence Green in *The Bookshop*, Annie Asra in *Human Voices*, and Hannah Graves in *At Freddie's* – with Fitzgerald's sense of herself: 'Nenna's character was faulty, but she had the instinct to see what made other people unhappy, and this instinct had only failed her once, in the case of her own husband' (*OF* 10–11). *Offshore's* Italian epigraph conveys some of the anguish: 'che mena il vento, e che batte la pioggia, / e che s'incontran con si aspre lingue' (Dante, *Inferno*, Canto 11), referring to those departed souls 'whom the wind drives, or whom the rain beats, or those who clash with such bitter tongues'. Written almost two decades after the events it portrays, *Offshore* presents life among the houseboat community as a tragicomedy arising from a particular situation. Fitzgerald observed that the instability of the craft moored on the reach, just yards from shore, embodied the 'emotional restlessness of my characters halfway between the need for security and the doubtful attraction of danger'.[22] This had been the Fitzgeralds' own situation when living on *Grace*. Out of instability was born success. *Offshore* made Fitzgerald's name when it won the Booker Prize in 1979, with the book lauded for its originality, honesty, and what Asa Briggs, the chairman of the judges, called its 'perpetual element of surprise' (*PF* 276).

In *Offshore*, typically for a Fitzgerald novel, story follows character. Will Nenna be reconciled with her estranged husband Edward? Will upright, decent Richard Blake be forced by his unhappy wife Laura to return to a life on land? Will the male prostitute Maurice, a warmly sympathetic figure, survive his dubious arrangement with Harry, a violent criminal? And will Nenna's daughters, Martha and Tilda, return to school?

Life itself may involve both choice and circumstance, but in *Offshore* plot and narrative suspense are driven chiefly by personality. Maurice, out of sheer amiability, allows Harry to store stolen goods on his boat. Nenna puts off visiting her husband at 42b Milvain Street because: 'it's my last chance. While I've still got it I can take it out and look at it and know I still have it. If that goes, I've nothing left to try' (*OF* 104). Yet Fitzgerald never simply disappears into her characters. Brief glimpses of the future, beyond the events of the novel, persuade us that the people we meet in *Offshore*'s pages actually exist, with real lives outside the story's brief telling: 'To his dying day the young Count would not forget the fair hand which had tended him when none other had heeded his plight' (*OF* 138). This is in part how Fitzgerald's short novels can appear to contain so much. 'Heinrich and Martha walked through this world, which was fated to last only a few years before the spell was broken, like a prince and princess' (*OF* 148). Historical hindsight generates pathos. We accompany the young couple through the bohemian playground of the King's Road in the early 1960s, and, simultaneously, look back on its disappearance decades later. The brief moment of Heinrich and Martha's happiness seems all the sweeter for belonging to a lost era. Elsewhere, as Nenna realizes just how far apart she and her husband Edward have drifted, such that it makes little difference whether she stays in London or moves to Nova Scotia, we hear the authoritative distillation of emotional truth from tragicomedy: 'All distances are the same to those who don't meet' (*OF* 165).

Each of the barge dwellers is pulled in two directions: land and water, head and heart, self and community. Each has 'the twofold need to take refuge and to escape' but no two characters feel the need in quite the same way (*PF* 148). Idiomatic speech distinguishes one from another. The hard-nosed businessman Pinkie speaks and thinks in public school slang: 'Poor old Richard, torpedoed three times, and then finished off, near as a toucher, with an adjustable spanner' (*OF* 169). The retired company director Woodrow uses City terms when thinking of old Willis, 'who must be getting on for sixty-five, ready to take the knock any day now' (*OF* 91). Richard's wife speaks in the snobbish county patois of her upbringing:

' "You can ask one or two of them to stay behind for a drink, if you like," Laura said, "if there's anyone possible"' (*OF* 7). And six-year old Tilda, an expert mimic, slips easily from 1960s teenspeak – '"Get outside this," she said, slamming the tin mug of coffee in front of him' (*OF* 138) – to the joyfully overwrought style of historical romance: 'Dear grandfather, are you sure you are not weary? Let us return to our ship. Take my arm, for though I am young, I am strong' (*OF* 59–60). Tilda's mother Nenna shows her age, and perhaps her sensibility, when explaining why they should wait to sell *Grace*: 'She's a thought damp. It would be easier in the spring' (*OF* 113). To use 'thought' in this way, as an adverb meaning 'a little' or 'a touch', marked a person out as belonging to a pre-1960s age.[23] Speech in the novel can also be silent. Both Nenna and Tilda carry on extensive interior monologues. Nenna tortures herself by imagining she is on trial for the failure of her marriage, culminating in the blunt, awful question: 'Mrs James. Do you like your husband?' (*OF* 39). Tilda's interior commentary, by contrast, is gloriously egotistical. During the bricking expedition with Martha, Tilda imagines herself as the star of the show:

> With a tile in each hand, balancing like a circus performer, Tilda returned. Under the garish lights of the Big Top, every man, woman and child rose to applaud. Who, they asked each other, was this newcomer, who had succeeded where so many others had failed? (*OF* 79)

A remarkably authentic sense of place and person is also established by Fitzgerald's style of narration, through deft touches of syntax, grammar, technical vocabulary, literary allusion, adages and ellipses. At the opening meeting of the boat dwellers, the maritime setting is instantly established by the elegant and nautically correct device of having each of the owners known by the name of his or her boat – *Lord Jim*, *Maurice*, *Grace*, *Dreadnought*. Seafaring terms add to the picture ('The tide was making', 'the flood was making fast' (*OF* 3–4, 24)), and the prose rhythm itself evokes an atmosphere blending both romance and reality: 'Between *Lord Jim*, moored almost in the shadow of Battersea Bridge and the old wooden Thames barges, two hundred yards upriver and close to the rubbish disposal wharfs and the brewery, there was a great gulf fixed' (*OF* 2). The terminal position in the sentence of the main clause ('there was a great gulf fixed') imitates poetic inversions of word order; the clause itself is unattributed biblical paraphrase, from Luke 16: 26: 'And besides all this, between us and you there is a great gulf fixed'. The combined effect is to enable us if not consciously to notice, then at least unconsciously to feel, the mythic potential in 'the mud moorings of the great tide-way'. The same understated appeal of the Thames to the heart is present in Richard's reveries – 'And if the river spoke to his dreaming, rather than to his daytime self, he supposed he had no business to attend to it' (*OF* 4) – where 'he supposed' conveys Richard's dutiful, 'daytime self' reluctantly pulling against the tidal dreamworld of the river.

Fitzgerald's narration is chameleon-like too in places, blurring the distinction between narrator and fictional character. 'With a faint smile the young Count turned to thank his saviour, while some colour stealed, stole back into his pale cheeks' (*OF* 139). The correction, mid-sentence, of 'stealed' to 'stole' gives the impression of a narrator or author thinking while in the very act of speaking or writing. It also imitates the young Austrian Count Heinrich's own manner of speaking. It is as though the narrator's mode of speech has been affected by Heinrich's – an oddly involuntary phenomenon most people have experienced in the presence of a foreign speaker or strong, distinctive accent. The effect of this strange kind of linguistic contagion is to make Heinrich seem all the more real by subtly showing us the effect he has on others, including even figures, such as the narrator, who stand outside the world of the novel.

In *Offshore* the narration is never intrusive, but nor is it invisible. Enigmatic assertion hints at personal experience: 'She was still at the RSM then, violin first study, and she fell in love as only a violinist can' (*OF* 35). Further questions are prompted by the conclusion of the impromptu party on Willis's boat:

> Encouraged, Willis offered to fetch mussels at once, and some plates and forks and vinegar, and switch on the radio while he was gone, to give them a bit of music. Woodie was surprised to learn that there were any plates on *Dreadnought*. 'May I have the first dance, Janet?' Maurice asked, up on his feet again. Couldn't he see that there was hardly room to sit? (*OF* 92)

Who is it that asks 'Couldn't he see'? The author or narrator? The other guests at the party? The imagined reader? Fitzgerald leaves us to wonder, but the effect of the question is to heighten the party's apparent reality, vividly evoking the feeling of being cramped, simply by assuming that *anyone*, had they been there, would have asked the same thing.

The verbal surface of *Offshore* is also enriched and enlivened by the presence of other words, other languages. Pop cultural references to Elvis Presley and Cliff Richard, and to *Bootsie and Snudge*, a popular British sit-com of the period, help to conjure up the almost mythical world of early 1960s London, 'fated to last only a few years before the spell was broken'. Favourite poetic points of reference connect this novel to Fitzgerald's next, *Human Voices*, which takes its title from T. S. Eliot's *Prufrock*. In *Offshore*, as Hermione Lee observes, Maurice and Nenna see the Thames as 'a powerful god, bearded with the white foam of detergents, calling home the twenty-seven lost rivers of London, sighing as the night declined', faintly echoing the Whitman-esque opening lines of Eliot's *Dry Salvages*: 'the river / Is a strong brown god – sullen, untamed and intractable' (*PF* 152). The German romantic poet Heinrich Heine (1797–1856), whose story 'Der Asra' provides the name of the central character in *Human Voices*, features too in *Offshore* when Heinrich consoles Martha: 'Listen, you are like the blonde mistress of Heine, the poet Heine, *wenig Fleisch, sehr viel Gemüt*, little body, but so much spirit' (*OF* 151). As readers we may not pick up on these allusions – Fitzgerald was disappointed when A. S. Byatt failed to do so (*PF* 74) – but we sense at least that *something* is going on, hovering tantalizingly just beyond understanding. In such a way, the overall allusive texture of Fitzgerald's novels, more than any specific reference or allusion, works diffusely, like the weather, to produce in the reader what Hans Ulrich Gumbrecht refers to as *Stimmungen*, particular moods or atmospheres evoked by aesthetic experience.[24]

Offshore was written in 1979, after Desmond's death, but it looks back to 1963, one of the lowest points in Fitzgerald's life. The emotional force of the novel clearly derives from Fitzgerald's complicated feelings about her marriage at that time and since, transmuted into fiction. 'Edward stayed in the Engineers for a bit, then came out and was not very successful in finding a job to suit him. That wasn't his fault, and if anyone said that it was, Nenna would still feel like poking a hole in them' (*OF* 35). The painful rawness of this is far from the emotional restraint and stylish equipoise for which Fitzgerald is usually praised. Nenna's fierce loyalty to Edward, despite all of his failings, makes for uncomfortable reading. The shame and disappointment arising from Desmond Fitzgerald's financial misdealings, about which his wife never spoke (*PF* 154–7), surely lies behind certain passages: 'The closing of the launderette had given rise to a case in the County Court, in which Edward and she had been held not to blame, but had been conscious of the contempt of their solicitor, who always seemed to be in a great hurry' (*OF* 36). Matters come to a head in Nenna and Eddie's impassioned but unhappy reunion at 42b Milvain Street:

> 'You don't have to stay there! There's plenty of jobs! Anyone can get a job anywhere!'
> 'I can't.'
> He turned his head away, and as the light caught his face at a certain angle Nenna realised in terror that he was right and that he would never get anywhere. The terror, however, was not for herself or for the children but for Edward, who might realise that what he was saying was true. (*OF* 115)

Here, more than in any other of her novels, Fitzgerald comes closest to portraying at least something of the lowest, most distressing moments of her fraught relationship with Desmond, recollected just four years after his death.

Offshore was admired in reviews, but the one that Fitzgerald cared about most was Frank Kermode's. He noted Fitzgerald's 'remarkable habit of accuracy, which shows not only in the wit of the book but in the provision, by apparently casual means, of a deep surface polish, an illusion of total specification...its texture a pure pleasure'. But he felt that *Offshore*, in comparison to *The Bookshop*, seemed 'anecdotal', 'the apocalyptic flood of the ending doesn't hold everything together'.[25] Fitzgerald wrote to Kermode, thanking him for his review, but also to say that what he referred to as the 'apocalyptic flood' wasn't 'really meant as apocalyptic...I only wanted the Thames to drift out a little way with the characters whom in the end nobody particularly wants or lays claim to. It seems to me that not to be wanted is a positive condition and I hoped to find some way of indicating that'.[26] Fitzgerald's defence is tactful and clear-minded in equal measure. Even so, Kermode is right: the ending of *Offshore* 'doesn't hold everything together', or at least not in the way that the endings of Fitzgerald's later novels do. (The same criticism might be levelled at the dark twist that ends *Human Voices*.) Yet in just fifty thousand words in *Offshore* Fitzgerald gives us so much, as Nenna begs Eddie to do, that such small points of criticism hardly signify. We understand that nothing in the barge dwellers' lives can stay the same, but this is far from saying that we accept the fact, returning only with reluctance to the world beyond the fictional one of the novel.

HUMAN VOICES (1980)

Human Voices was the third of Fitzgerald's novels to draw closely on her experience of work. The novel follows the lives of BBC staff at Broadcasting House during the Blitz of 1940, vividly evoking an idiosyncratic institution and its stubborn insistence on telling the truth, however damaging that might be to national morale.[27] Rule-bound, intensely ritualistic communities such as the BBC fascinated Fitzgerald, and telling the truth (or, at least, not telling lies) was always important to her.[28] Her work is full of uncompromising truth-tellers such as her uncle, Wilfred Knox, Pierce Carroll in *At Freddie's*, and straight-talking children like Christine Gipping in *The Bookshop* or Dolly Reid in *The Beginning of Spring*. Yet the title of *Human Voices* does not refer only and high-mindedly to those noble, measured, candid voices broadcasting to a darkened Europe. It also alludes to what interested Fitzgerald above all, the ceaseless human need to hear and be heard: 'There was always time for conversations of this kind, and of every kind, at Broadcasting House...[all] talking, talking to each other, and usually about each other, until the very last moment when the notice SILENCE: ON THE AIR forbade' (*HV* 5–6). But there is still more to *Human Voices* than both a tribute to the BBC and a celebration of the human desire to communicate. Its title also alludes darkly to the concluding, anti-romantic lines of T. S. Eliot's *The Love Song of J. Alfred Prufrock*:

> We have lingered in the chambers of the sea
> By sea-girls wreathed with seaweed red and brown
> Till human voices wake us, and we drown.

Eliot reminds us that the world of the imagination, of art and idealism, can only keep us for so long, before reality intrudes and we return tragically to the human realm. *Human Voices*, then, not only takes us back to the offices and corridors of Broadcasting House in 1940. It also asks profound questions about reality and unreality, what it is to be absorbed in art or idealism, music, sound or love.

Fitzgerald herself summed up the novel: 'It is really about the love-hate relationship between 2 of the eccentrics on whom the BBC depended, and about love, jealousy, death, childbirth in Broadcasting House and the crises that go on behind the microphone to produce the 9 o'clock news on which the whole nation relied during the war years, heartbreak &c, and also about this truth telling business.'[29] One of the eccentrics is the indispensable man-child Sam Brooks, the BBC's Recorded Programmes Director (RPD), possibly based on H. Lynton Fletcher, then Head of Recorded Programmes (*PF* 74–5). The other is the sardonic Director of Programme Planning (DPP), Jeffrey Haggard, whose second wife left him 'because, as she told her lawyers, she could never make him raise his voice' (*HV* 26).[30] The odd-couple friendship between RPD and DPP, with Jeff the parent and Sam the child, produces rich ironies, apparent both to the reader and to the characters themselves. Jeff tries to explain the friendship to himself:

> Their long relationship looked like an addiction – a weakness for the weak on Jeff's part – or a response to the appeal for protection made by the defenceless and single-minded. Of course, if this appeal were to fail entirely, the human race would have difficulty in reproducing itself. (*HV* 26)

Narration and free indirect speech, finely balanced throughout, become indistinguishable in the final sentence here, which belongs equally to the narrator and to Jeff. The effect is a double one: bringing Jeff fully to life while also imbuing the narrative voice with its own distinct personality.

Though both RPD and DPP are well drawn, neither occupies the novel's central role. Annie Asra, Fitzgerald's *alter ego*, has that honour but doesn't appear until two-thirds of the way through the book, though soon we know more about Annie than about any other character in the novel. Annie's widower father had been a piano tuner in Birmingham, taking his young daughter with him on his rounds: 'When he at last took out his hammer and mutes, ready to tune, his daughter became quite still, like a small dog pointing' (*HV* 84). When Annie was sixteen, her father had died. Quietly, purposefully, Annie sets off to try her luck in London and is interviewed at Broadcasting House by Jeff and Sam, and Mrs Milne and Mrs Staples 'from Establishment'. Mrs Milne explains what the job would entail:

> 'you would be working on shift – you'll have to take that into account, by the way, when you're finding somewhere to live – and you're not likely to have much direct contact with Mr Brooks.' Annie didn't miss the change from *you would* to *you will*, and she observed with compassion that Mrs Milne looked downright tired. (*HV* 92)

This brief exchange, as Fitzgerald intends, yields a high dividend: developing plot, giving voice to minor characters, and showing Annie's astuteness and feeling for others. Fitzgerald herself commented: 'as I'm a hopelessly addicted writer of short books I have to see to it that every confrontation and every dialogue has some reference to what I hope will be understood as the heart of the novel' (*HA* 517).

Fitzgerald expects her readers to be perceptive too. Some characters are clearly described by their names: Haggard, Staples, Vogel (or 'Bird'), Waterlow. But the meaning of 'Asra' is less obvious. '"My last head teacher told me it was the name of a tribe," said Annie. "I thought that was going a bit far"' (*HV* 106). Neither Annie nor anyone else in the novel knows that the name alludes to Heinrich Heine's poem 'Der Asra', about a tribe of slaves who die when they love ('welche sterben, wenn sie lieben'). But Fitzgerald assumes that the reader *will* know, thereby setting up dramatic irony about Annie's fate.[31] Events come to a head when RPD takes his juniors out to a celebratory dinner at Prunier's. Fitzgerald brilliantly evokes the heady atmosphere with the deftest of strokes: 'Their Director gave them all a little more champagne, ignoring the just imperceptible hint not to do this, sketched by the retreating waiter. The infants are getting over-excited, his shoulders said' (*HV* 129).

Part of the delight of this is that the French waiter's shoulders not only speak (silently), but do so in a French version of English, incorrectly translating 'infants' from the French 'enfants' (children). Sam makes a ring out of an inch of gold wire and a red currant and puts it on the third finger of Annie's left hand:

> The others watched in silence. Annie did not know what to say or do, so she said nothing, and left her hand where it was on the table. Something inside her seemed to move and unclose.... At that precise moment, while the juniors were eating their dessert at Prunier's, Annie fell in love with RPD absolutely, and hers must have been the last generation to fall in love without hope in such an unproductive way. (*HV* 131–2)[32]

It is at this precise moment, more than two-thirds of the way through its length, that the novel springs fully into life. Annie's ensuing feelings and experience only reinforce the identification of her fate with 'Der Asra'. She thinks about Sam Brooks's loneliness following Mrs Brooks's departure: 'but then you couldn't really pretend that he was lonely, and so Annie didn't pretend. This, of course, meant that she suffered twice, and she failed to reckon the extra costs of honesty' (*HV* 132–3). Fitzgerald's emotional accounting here is characteristically exacting. Annie not only falls in love without hope, but does so without deluding herself that she was needed.

Minor characters, as always in Fitzgerald's fiction, are fully imagined. Jack Barnett, of Transport, Supply and Equipment, leaps off the page: 'If you can tell me where to get any more steel filing cabinets measuring up to our specifications, Mr Haggard, I'm prepared to go to bed with Hitler's grandmother' (*HV* 146). Practical people and problem-solvers, however harassed, are always treated warmly in Fitzgerald's novels. At the same time, middle-class attitudes and values are the target for gentle satire. Mrs Milne and Mrs Staples agree on the domestic priority items to save from the bombs:

> 'You mean specimen glass and china, and that sort of thing?'
> 'Yes, the irreplaceables, the things you never use – those are what really matters.' (*HV* 144)

Dialogue here treads a fine line. The reader smiles at Mrs Milne's and Mrs Staples's shared certainty about the value of 'the things you never use', but stops short of impugning them for it. The trick of this lies, in part, in Mrs Staples's ungrammatical but idiomatic use of 'matters'. Individual character lies in such habits of speech, and the reader's interest and sympathy with it. Sometimes such characterization is achieved indirectly, when the narrator slips into the mode of speech of the person described: 'Mac flung down a large sack of oranges and threw his arms round Jeff, as when brave and reluctantly friendly paleface meet' (*HV* 61). This idiom – derived from Western novels and movies – belongs to Mac rather than the narrator. It reinforces our sense of Mac as a living, breathing person who appear to influence the narrator's manner of speech (just as Heinrich seems to do in *Offshore*). At other times, comic characters seem to exist independent of any creator, so audibly polished are the rhythms and inverted syntax of their patter. Enter the old performer Fred Shotto, standing in for his son. He declares: 'He's Fred Shotto, junior. You can bill me as the old block he's a chip of' (*HV* 101).

Fitzgerald shows how this unruly babel was held together, ennobled even, by the BBC's commitment to truth. Her narrative voice takes on a retrospective, oratorical, far-reaching quality:

> As an institution that could not tell a lie, they were unique in the contrivances of gods and men since the Oracle of Delphi. As office managers, they were no more than adequate, but now, as autumn approached, with the exiles crowded awkwardly into their new sections, they were broadcasting in the strictest sense of the word, scattering human voices into the darkness of Europe, in the certainty that more than half must be lost, some for the rook, some for the crow, for the sake of a few that made their mark. And everyone who worked there, bitterly complaining about the short-sightedness of their colleagues, the vanity of the news readers, the remoteness of the Controllers and the restrictive nature of the canteen's one teaspoon, felt a certain pride which they had no way to express, either then or since. (*HV* 103)

The balance of this passage is remarkable – between pride and complaint, order and chaos – the long, multi-clausal sentences infused with voices from the classical past and folklore. In the old planting rhyme, men sang 'one for the rook, one for the crow' as they sowed, knowing that some of the seed would be lost.[33] This is precisely appropriate here given that the BBC was 'broadcasting in the strictest sense of the word', 'scattering' human voices like seed 'into the darkness of Europe'.

Yet for all its appreciation of the BBC's worth, *Human Voices* is searingly critical of the self-importance of its senior managers. The focus for this criticism is the defeatist broadcast by the exiled French General Pinard. Realizing what Pinard is about to say, Jeff takes the drastic step of 'pulling the plugs'. As a result, Pinard's speech is not broadcast but the network is silent for ten minutes. Haggard is dressed down for taking matters into his own hands; the ire of BBC senior management is only inflamed by Churchill's approval of Jeff's action. Later, when the BBC's Assistant Deputy Director General (ADDG) had come to realize just how much Jeff was needed to keep the place running:

> ADDG, with the leniency of someone who has been unjust in the first place, considered that Haggard's nerves might have been overtaxed.... 'I think I'll advise him to read a few chapters of *Cranford* every night before he retires to bed. I've been doing that myself ever since Munich. I think, you know, that Mrs Gaskell would have been glad to know that.' (*HV* 44)

This is a perfect example of Fitzgerald's creation of speech out of context that leaves the reader guessing. To whom is ADDG speaking? His wife, in a domestic setting? To the Director General or another Old Servant, more formally? To himself? This uncertainty only heightens the supremely Pooterish complacency of ADDG's speech, which surely owes a comic debt to Fitzgerald's love for the Grossmiths' *Diary of a Nobody*. But however much *Cranford* Jeff reads, he will never quite belong. ADDG, when writing Jeff's obituary, is doubtful as to whether he should describe Jeff as an Old Servant, in spite of all he had done for the BBC: 'Even after so many years, he seemed hardly that' (*HV* 200). These final lines of the book, in their ironic voicing of the condescension of the BBC's senior management, are as bitterly disillusioned as any in Fitzgerald's work, even coming close to the desolate ending of *The Bookshop*.

Structurally, *Human Voices* is a curiosity. At the level of sentence, paragraph and scene it is remarkably self-assured, brilliantly evocative, funny and sad. But taken as a whole, the most fully fleshed-out character, Annie Asra, appears only very late on, individual storylines don't quite cohere, and the manner of Jeff Haggard's death is arguably a misstep, straying closer to farce than tragedy, not unlike the ending of *Offshore*. Reviewers have noted these imperfections of design, seeing in *Human Voices* the scrambled frequencies of different wavelengths, coming in and out of tune: 'It is all scrappy, voices rising and falling, moments focussed and their consequences lost.' Yet, as A. S. Byatt observes, the scrappiness, silences and absences are not extrinsic to the work, but 'part of the theme and method' of the novel.[34] That theme and method, of voices rising and falling, are exemplified in the remarkable scene when Annie declares her feelings for Sam. Sam, realization dawning, proposes that they go and have a drink and 'start from the beginning'.

> Her happiness was greater than she could bear.
> 'That'll be very nice.'
> 'It won't be all that nice,' said Sam, feeling compunction, and amazement at himself for feeling it.... Their lives were shaking into pieces. 'What are we going to do, Annie?' he asked in bewilderment. She put her arms round him. Good-bye, Asra, she thought. God knows what's going to become of you now. (*HV* 194)

The reader 'hears' Annie's thoughts, but does she in fact say anything in response to Sam's question? It is wholly consistent with Fitzgerald's portrayal in *Human Voices* of the unending human need to communicate, that at this bewildering moment of happiness Annie should choose not to speak but to act. It is in keeping too with Fitzgerald's uncanny instinct of knowing when 'to let the voices fall silent', reminding us in a novel not only full of but also about those voices, as Fitzgerald says of Dickens and Jane Austen, 'that one of the privileges of dialogue is silence' (*HA* 505, 507).

AT FREDDIE'S (1982)

Fitzgerald's fifth novel draws on her experience of teaching at the Italia Conti stage school in the early 1960s. It follows the lives of the owner of the Temple Stage School, Frieda or 'Freddie' Wentworth, of two pupils, Mattie Stewart and Jonathan Kemp, and two teachers, Pierce Carroll and Hannah

Graves. Like Hannah, Fitzgerald taught general subjects (arithmetic and spelling) to fiercely resistant stage school pupils.[35] For its portrait of Freddie, the book also draws in part on Fitzgerald's memory of the doughty, cajoling founder of Westminster Tutors, Miss Freeston. The school's premises smelled of old leather and 'decaying dogs' and Fitzgerald imbued Freddie both with Miss Freeston's domineering character and distinctive aroma. As Fitzgerald commented to her editor Richard Ollard: 'all the characters are taken straight from life, whether successfully or not'.[36] This slightly exasperated remark was provoked by a hostile review; of all of her novels, *At Freddie's* is the one that most divides the critics. For some, the book is 'one of the tiny handful of great theatre novels, up there with Michael Blakemore's *Next Season*, Priestley's *Lost Empires* and Michael Redgrave's *The Mountebank's Tale*.[37] For others, the novel is sentimental, *faux-naif*, and 'instantly forgettable'.[38]

It is hard to understand why readers should be so sharply at odds. *At Freddie's* contains all the trademark qualities of Fitzgerald's fiction: precise observation of people and places, understated wit, equal measures of comedy and sadness, narrative unpredictability punctuated, in this case, by insights into the magic of theatrical illusion. The authoritative narrator's voice immediately establishes the physical reality of the place: 'Everyone who knew the Temple School will remember the distinctive smell of Freddie's office' (*AF* 4). Freddie herself, an amalgam of Miss Freeston and Lilian Baylis, the ferociously iron-willed manager of the Old Vic, is richly plausible in her contradictions, rudeness and cunning: 'And Freddie continued to withhold, from her store of unforgivable remarks, the insult which might part them for ever' (*AF* 71). Finely observed patterns of speech individualize each character:

> 'That's a bold child, that Mattie Stewart,' Carroll observed, and at the word 'bold', which you'd never hear used in that way in England, both of them were taken back together over many years. Without thinking she put her arm through his. (*AF* 131)

In the case here of the Belfast Catholic Hannah Graves and the 'black Protestant' Pierce Carroll, from rural Northern Ireland, speech both individualizes *and* brings characters together.

It is the morose Pierce who makes the deepest impression on Freddie, telling her: ' "It's a great mistake to live with the past victories." ...Freddie felt some interest in Carroll, more, perhaps, than in Hannah. She had heard in his remarks the weak, but pure, voice of complete honesty' (*AF* 23). Too much honesty though can be as unsettling as too little, as Hannah realizes after Pierce proposes to her: 'At this point it came to her that she was not good enough for Pierce, and nobody can bear this feeling for any length of time' (*AF* 207). Later they revisit the moment of his proposal. Pierce asks:

> 'Did you think that I ought to have said more than I did about my feelings?'
> 'No.'
> 'You resented that, perhaps.'
> 'No, not at all.'
> 'I was afraid you might not have done.' (*AF* 210)

Pierce's worst fears are confirmed. His proposal to Hannah had left her so unmoved that she hadn't even felt affronted.

Such sharply observed emotional interplay in *At Freddie's* acquires a more generalized resonance through the book's atmosphere of literary allusion, quotation and performance. Yet rarely is a literary echo or quotation overtly signalled or explained as such. Freddie deigns to speak, in the company of Freddie's accountant, Unwin, to the businessman Joey Blatt, who wants to invest in the stage school. The nine-year-old boy actor Jonathan interrupts the meeting.

> 'Mr Blatt has come to tell me that I don't know how to run my own business,' Freddie went on.
> 'Oh, surely that can't be so, Miss Wentworth.'
> 'He says he wants to help the school. He's anxious to give me some money.'
> 'What is money?' Jonathan asked.
> 'Now look here, son,' said Blatt, 'you know what money is.'
> Unwin felt that if no one else was going to put a stop to this, he must, particularly when the little boy went on, in a sleepy whisper that chilled the blood, 'Money isn't cruel, is it? But if it isn't cruel, why didn't it save my mother?' (*AF* 68)

For a moment the tone skews wildly towards a strange kind of tragic pathos. But the full, deferred pleasure of this only becomes apparent eight pages later when we learn in passing that Jonathan's words belong to a song from a musical version of *Dombey & Son*, a song that all the child actors know. Fitzgerald uses quotation here for purely comic purposes, and to discomfort Joey Blatt (and the unwary reader for a time too). Elsewhere in the novel an allusion to Prospero's 'We are such stuff / As dreams are made on' speech in *The Tempest* works to define the limits of a character's sympathies. Speaking of the theatre, Hannah asks Pierce 'whether he didn't find it rather sad to see human beings giving a lifetime's concentration to what must melt into air, into thin air.'

> 'I think that's a bit from Shakespeare you've got there,' Pierce had said.
> 'Well, yes.'
> 'If you ask me, he was a bit of a showman.' (*AF* 187)

Pierce's clumsily honest but wholly inadequate response, shutting down further discussion, swiftly and sadly tells us all that we need to know. There can be no chance for Hannah and Pierce.

Other almost imperceptible literary echoes contribute to the book's particular atmosphere of artistic propensities suppressed and unrealized. Fitzgerald describes how Mattie's father feels about Freddie's financial management of the school: 'At the very idea of profits going to waste, even if they didn't concern him directly, he felt a mixture of wistfulness and anger, like a poet conscious of all the roses that fall' (*AF* 62). This is an unexpectedly poignant comparison, between the preoccupations of a prosperous chain-store owner and the mind of 'a poet'. But there is an echo too, in 'all the roses that fall', of the words of the Irish song 'Oh Danny Boy', distantly but recognizably reminiscent of Pierce's futile love for Hannah: 'The summer's gone, and all the roses falling / It's you, it's you must go and I must bide'. What might have been a merely localized moment of characterization becomes, through its half-perceived connection to Hannah and Pierce, something that belongs to the larger romantic sensibility that pervades the whole novel.

At Freddie's is particularly brilliant on theatrical illusion, on its unlikely magic and appeal. Fitzgerald's own keen theatre-going animates her picture of Londoners heading to the West End:

At this very moment they were hurrying off from work, bolting their macaroni cheese (Freddie's heart was always with the cheaper seats) and braving the struggle back into the city, to concentrate on what was said and done in a lighted frame, which, when it went dark, would make them cry to dream again. They were creators in their own right, each performance coming to life, if it ever did, between the actors and the audience, and after that lost for eternity. The extravagance of that loss was its charm. (*AF* 73)

Fitzgerald had always been beguiled by the stage. Forty years earlier, she had reviewed Herbert Farjeon's revue *Light and Shade*: 'The theatre gives you a new world, one that seems real if the play is successful, but a different world. Out of cardboard and plaster, out of intonations and tricks with time, the theatre creates this astonishing illusion.'[39] Just as, she might have added, fiction does out of words, inflections, echoes and whispers, what is said and not said, heard and not heard. Fitzgerald's longstanding fascination with the theatre was not only an aesthetic or philosophical one, but a technical and artistic one too. She loved to know how things were done, how such illusions were created. In *At Freddie's* Fitzgerald's interest in stagecraft focuses on actors in particular, and on those rare moments when one 'achieved the moment of electrifying contact with the audience in front of him which may only once or twice in a lifetime be the actor's reward' (*AF* 175). Some actors, such as Mattie Stewart, destined to be a movie star, possess mere imitative facility, trained up to competence. Others, such as the boy-genius Jonathan Kemp, work intuitively, interested almost wholly in technique and barely at all in psychology: 'Jonathan was born to be one of those actors who work from the outside inwards. To them, the surface is not superficial. He didn't want to know what it felt like to be desperate enough to jump from a wall; he wanted to know what someone looked like when they did' (*AF* 101).

The essence of Jonathan's art is obsessive, single-minded concentration. Due to take the role of Prince Arthur in *King John*, in which the prince dies when jumping to escape from imprisonment, Jonathan realizes that he must practise the jump in the little walled yard behind the school. He approaches first Freddie and then Pierce for help, but both are preoccupied with their own affairs. Doggedly, Jonathan persists on his own, dragging rotten fruit crates from Covent Garden to enable him to climb onto the wall. By now, late in the evening, Jonathan has been locked out of the school and faces a worryingly long drop from the wall to the street to get out. 'Still, he had other resources', observes the narrator, and Jonathan remains undisturbed and intent on his aim, which 'was to get so used to the jump that he could do it without thinking, and exactly the same way every time'. He anticipates the morning, when someone would come and tell him 'whether he was right or not'. The book closes, snow swirling, with Jonathan determined to get it right. 'Meanwhile he went on climbing and jumping, again and again and again into the darkness' (*AF* 230). No single image is as ominous in all of Penelope Fitzgerald's fiction.

Fitzgerald explained in an interview that she had meant Jonathan to die, or for the reader to think that he would die, accidentally, leaping off the wall. 'But nobody has grasped this, she added, and that was her fault.'[40] Criticism of *At Freddie's* centres on Fitzgerald's perceived affection for her characters, the seemingly arch or knowing narration and dialogue, and the sense that not enough is at stake. Yet, as its enigmatic, unsettling ending shows, the book is far darker than such critics suppose, and not at all 'well mannered' as one reviewer put it. It also contains moments of pure uproarious joy, such as the boy-dancer Gianni's outraged riposte to Hannah:

> 'Christ, Miss, you don't believe me. I'm not a liar. I'm not going in for acting, you know that, I'm a dancer, my style's hat and cane like Frankie Vaughan, Frankie's given untold sums to selected charities.' (*AF* 58)

This last phrase – 'untold sums to selected charities' – is comic dialogue of the highest order; the promotional language of the press release put in the mouth of a child. If the novel has a weakness it is that Hannah Graves, unlike Florence Green, Nenna James or even Annie Asra, never quite comes sufficiently to life. The reader is privy to her thoughts and emotions – 'he had never so much as called round at her place again, and she thought the more of him for that, or perhaps, to be honest, she thought less' (*AF* 207) – but Hannah is never really troubled by Pierce, or Boney Lewis, her actor lover, or by Freddie. Life never seems to cost her quite enough. As a result, Pierce becomes the emotional focus of the novel. He tells Miss Blewett that he had asked Hannah to marry him. 'Miss Blewett caught his expression and without hesitation folded him, as he stood there in his second best homegoing tweed, in her arms' (*AF* 150). Yet because Pierce is so doomed and Hannah so resilient and self-reliant the emotional energy of the novel is dissipated rather than concentrated. But such a slight imbalance is a small price to pay for the 'pure gold' of this constantly surprising, deeply moving, yet most underrated and misunderstood of Fitzgerald's early novels.

4

Late Novels

In the decade following the publication of *Charlotte Mew and Her Friends* (1984), Penelope Fitzgerald wrote a remarkable quartet of novels: *Innocence* (1986), *The Beginning of Spring* (1988), *The Gate of Angels* (1990) and *The Blue Flower* (1995). Set in Italy, Russia, England and Germany, and ranging in time from the late-eighteenth to the mid-twentieth century, these four works are often described as 'historical novels' as though history were the most important thing about them. But Fitzgerald herself disliked the term, pointing out that 'All novels, in fact, are historical'.[1] By this she meant that novels only tell stories about things that have already happened (even Orwell's *Nineteen Eighty-Four* and Huxley's *Brave New World* are told in the past tense); and also, more formally, that the novel, like music and drama, is a temporal art form unfolding in time and history. I prefer, then, to call these four works Fitzgerald's 'late' rather than historical novels, partly because history is decidedly *not* what defines them, and partly to signal their difference – less autobiographical, more boldly experimental in narrative form and style, and even more intensely concerned with profound questions of body, mind and spirit – from Fitzgerald's 'early' novels.[2]

These four late works are the peak of Fitzgerald's achievement as a writer. *The Beginning of Spring* and *The Gate of Angels* were shortlisted for the Booker Prize, and *The Blue Flower*, unaccountably overlooked for the Booker, won the US National Book Critics' Circle Award. All four have been praised for their uncanny evocation of particular times and places, for their structural economy and innovation, for their bodying forth of big ideas about life, death and the nature of reality in the guise of stories of romance and mystery. In these novels, in which fictional characters mingle with famous names from history, including Antonio Gramsci, Tolstoy, Ernest Rutherford, Goethe, Fichte and Schiller, Fitzgerald ranges far beyond the experiences of her own life. Yet perhaps not so far, upon closer inspection. The plots of all four novels present versions of thwarted desire: Fred's epiphanic longing for Daisy in *The Gate of Angels*; Salvatore and Chiara's tempestuous love story in *Innocence*; Frank's craving for Lisa in *The Beginning of Spring*, or at least his desire for something other than his marriage; Fritz's idealized yearning both for Sophie, his 'heart's heart', and for revelation in *The Blue Flower*. The traces of Fitzgerald's own experiences, especially of her often difficult marriage, are more or less discernible in each of these situations, and are the mostly undetected wellsprings of the distinctive quality of sympathy for human needs and weakness that pervades these late works.

Yet, autobiographical resonances apart, the question remains: how does she do it? How in these last novels does Fitzgerald deploy the devices of narrative art to create fictional worlds, alien to her own experience and upbringing, that expand to inhabit the reader's imagination and even appear to possess an existence independent of the novels themselves; whose characters, in their courage, absurdity and intimacy with the author ('the central people in Penelope Fitzgerald novels seem to share her sense of humour')[3] appear as real to us as ourselves; stories whose opacities and mysteries hint at shadowy realms beyond their telling, dimly perceived and achingly out of reach? 'Obliquity, timing, and the virtues of omission and allusion are her secrets,' Michael Dibdin observed,[4] and this chapter shows how these stylistic features combine to produce the magical effects of each novel. Other contrivances also play a part. Subtle shifts in narrative perspective prompt the question, 'who is telling me this story?', disturbing, but at the same time deepening, the reader's involvement in the fiction. Syntax and diction that insinuate not only specific moods but appear to emanate from the characters themselves, even when they are silent, conjure the immediacy of the eye-witness account. Literary echoes, quotations and paraphrases – barely registered or understood – generate a specific ambience or atmosphere in each novel, in which allusions, 'always a return', align the use of fiction with the use of memory.[5] Such aspects of Fitzgerald's craft are common to all of her last four novels, but the privilege of analysis is to show how they are freshly applied in each case, and in different measures and patterns according to the precise emotional, intellectual and technical needs of each novel, achieving startlingly different effects in the process.

INNOCENCE (1986)

For the world of *Innocence*, her first novel set abroad, Fitzgerald turned to the Italy of the mid-1950s, a time and a place she knew well. In 1949 she and Desmond had had a belated honeymoon in Rome, and in the early 1950s in *World Review* they had published short stories by contemporary Italian writers: Alberto Moravia, Mario Soldati, Guglielmo Petroni and Giorgio Bassani, among others. Fitzgerald visited Italy many times: to Urbino in the Apennines to stay with her cousin Oliver Knox, to Venice for a PEN conference, and frequently to Florence (*PF* 309). One such trip seems to have been the genesis of *Innocence*. According to Fitzgerald, she visited Florence one spring 'with the idea of identifying the flowers in Botticelli's *Primavera*, and found herself instead absorbed in the marital squabbling of a contessa with whom she was lodging and her doctor husband from the south of Italy'. The seed was planted for a story about 'people who don't fit too well – as many don't, I suppose'.[6] The squabbling couple appears in *Innocence* hardly changed, as a Florentine contessina (eighteen-year-old Chiara Ridolfi) and a southern Italian doctor (Salvatore Rossi, 'thirtyish'), fiercely attracted to one another yet scarcely able to co-exist. One is tidy, decisive, impatient and intolerant, the other messy, uncertain, selfless and kind. Both are impulsive and highly strung. They argue incessantly, but 'Perhaps we might agree about everything, Salvatore thought. No-one ever agrees with me, but she might' (*IN* 42). Clearly, the setting and dramatis personae of *Innocence* announce it as the beginning of a new, non-autobiographical phase in Fitzgerald's fiction. Yet the novel does contain one unheralded though poignant parallel with Fitzgerald's own life: like Fitzgerald, 'Chiara miscarried and the baby's doubtful experiment came to nothing' (*IN* 292). Such moments hint at a more pervasive identification between author and story than is usually recognized. Indeed, Fitzgerald could hardly have imagined Chiara and Salvatore's combustible relationship without thinking of her own. If 'people who don't fit too well' is the given situation in *Innocence*, then the novel's theme – 'what a great mistake it is to try and make other people happy' (*PF* 308) – can best be understood in relation to its enigmatic title. The events of the novel show that trying to make other people happy is naive, childlike, innocent of reality. At the furthest extreme, as in the legend with which the novel begins, the charitable impulse even leads to blinding and mutilation. The story leaps forward to the twentieth century, yet the family trait somehow persists: 'Still a tendency towards rash decisions, perhaps, always intended to ensure other people's happiness, once and for all' (*IN* 10). Both Chiara and Marta (Salvatore's mistress) try in different ways to make Salvatore happy, but succeed only in incensing him:

> It struck him that both Marta and Chiara took advantage of him by attacking him with their ignorance, or call it innocence. A serious thinking adult had no defence against innocence because he was obliged to respect it, whereas the innocent scarcely knows what respect is, or seriousness either. (*IN* 205)

In Salvatore's eyes, Marta and Chiara, and Chiara's Aunt Mad too, are infuriatingly innocent (or ignorant) because in wishing to make him happy they undermine his fiercely held boyhood resolution that 'he would be emotionally dependent on no one' (*IN* 62). The women have forgotten, or chosen not to remember, that it is often easier to give than receive. Just as fiercely, Salvatore had resolved never to concern himself with politics, nor to give his health or life for his beliefs. This gives rise to a further perspective on innocence in the novel. From Salvatore's point of view, the Communist writer and leader Antonio Gramsci and his followers, Sannazarro and Domenico (Salvatore's father), are culpably innocent for their misguided loyalty to a political ideal. Salvatore is not anti-Communist; he just thinks of himself as dealing with the world as it is and not as it might be. One further, more profound sense of innocence arises due to the thirty-year interval between the events of the story and their telling. Even the figures seemingly most accommodated or resigned to the ways of the world – Chiara's father Giancarlo, her cousin Cesare, and her uncle, Monsignor Gondi – come to seem ingenuous, unknowing and as vulnerable to time and fate as anyone else as three decades later the narrator looks back on their lives. Hindsight is ruthless or kind depending on how you look at it, rendering everyone in life, in fiction, and even in reading fiction, foolish or innocent. By the end of a novel, no reader is quite the same, nor sees things in quite the same way as at the beginning.

Innocence is the most inconclusive and oblique, yet curiously bewitching, of all Fitzgerald's novels. Praised for the remarkable authenticity of its depiction of Florence in the 1950s, for its sinuous presentation in its characters of the coexistence of innocence and cunning, suffering and happiness ('precious, painful and euphoric'), and for its 'strange, muted power and intelligence', *Innocence* achieves three effects in particular which, in combination, exert a powerful hold over the reader.[7] First the creation of characters whose personalities not only seem manifestly real in their contradictions and unpredictability, but whose lives, seemingly existing independently of the novel, appear poised between unavoidable fate and uncertain freedom. Second the creation of a fictional world that appears to be history rather than make-believe, rapidly inhabiting the mind of the reader. And third, the generation of a mounting yet indefinable sense that the story, in its hints at deep causal and ironic connections between past and present, character and fate, the individual and the universal, contains more than meets the eye. In part, these effects are achieved in *Innocence* through Fitzgerald's habitual method of narrative distillation and ellipsis. Anticipating the episodic structure of *The Blue Flower*, some chapters in *Innocence* are just a paragraph long, concentrating drama, condensing space, time and information. Yet three principal interconnected novelistic devices – shifts in time and narrative viewpoint, multipersonal presentation of consciousness, and intertextual density – stand out as the means by which Fitzgerald achieves the particular moods, cross-currents and pathos of this novel.

Two structural time shifts persuade us that this is a story that actually happened. At the outset, the narrative leap from the Ridolfis of the sixteenth century to those of the twentieth intensifies the realism of the latter. In contrast to the Gothic legend of the midget Ridolfis, even the most absurd moments in Fitzgerald's depiction of 1950s Italy seem plausible. The second time shift is an instance of prolepsis in which the reader is made aware of Chiara's impending marriage to Salvatore early in the novel. When a hundred and fifty pages later the wedding actually takes place, the reader, having known it was coming, stands both in and outside of the story, in a privileged position close to that of the author. Prolepsis is a familiar enough narrative device, but Fitzgerald's brilliance lies in concealing the precise moment when the story tracks back, to Chiara and Salvatore's courtship, rather than forwards in time – the temporal equivalent of an M. C. Escher drawing. Other instances of prolepsis offer glimpses of a future beyond the end of the novel. Musing aloud on the Ridolfis' rash attempts to make people happy, the narrator remarks: 'It seems an odd characteristic to survive for so many years. Perhaps it won't do so for much longer' (*PF* 10). By its mere hint at the future, the reader is prompted to imagine the lives of Chiara and Salvatore, and of their children, going on long after the brief span of the 1950s story. This is precisely what Fitzgerald intends. The marriage plot, 'the bourne of so many narratives', is only the beginning of the story in *Innocence*. What happens after marriage is where the author's and reader's interest really lies. Other tiny portents are planted sparingly elsewhere. Chiara's English friend Barney, astoundingly, marries Toby Harrington, telling Chiara the news on the phone from London. The changed state of their friendship (and not for the better) that this news betokens is captured in Barney's change in tone, 'calmly dismissive, the voice of authority. "You must let us know, though, if you're ever in Chipping Camden."' In response, the narrator suddenly looks forward, picturing Chiara many years hence: 'But during the later stages of her life, at times when things were not going well for her, the bewildering phrase used to come back to her without warning: You must let us know, though, if ever you're in Chipping Camden' (*IN* 294). The poignant, tragicomic effect of this, so characteristic of Fitzgerald's fiction, arises from the combination of the unexpected glimpse into the future and the sudden saddening change in a friendship. The melancholy irony of gigantic, endearing Barney becoming the coolly conventionally middle-class English hostess is only sharpened by Fitzgerald's use of reported speech to show Chiara recalling her friend's mystifying words. Like Dickens, Fitzgerald knew precisely the moment to let her characters fall silent.

Sudden shifts in narrative viewpoint serve both to settle and disturb the realistic surface of the novel. Seemingly, the story is recalled in the very moment of its telling: 'He was young,' the narrator says of Salvatore – then corrects herself mid-stream, 'not so very young, thirtyish, a specialist at the S. Agostino Hospital, clever, very hard-working'. By representing her narrator as someone who wryly corrects herself mid-sentence, the better to tell the truth, Fitzgerald achieves an effect quite opposite to that of Virginia Woolf in the famous brown stocking passage in *To the Lighthouse*. Woolf's narrator hesitates and doubts in order to achieve the Modernist effect of 'obscuring or even obliterating the impression of an objective reality completely known to the author'.[8] The self-adjustments of Fitzgerald's narrator, by contrast, bring her into closer intimacy with her characters, and strengthen the impression of a reality completely known to the author. The feeling that we are listening to someone who knows the characters themselves, who inhabits their world, is made palpable by what comes straight after: '"Hard-working, I suppose that means he's from the South," said Maddalena' (*IN* 10). Uncannily, Chiara's Aunt Mad seems to respond directly to the narrator's words, as though they had been addressed to her, or as though she had overheard them being addressed to the reader. Who exactly, we wonder, is telling this story? The mystery of the narrator's identity is only deepened by the kind of time shifts discussed above. The narrator's account of Chiara and Salvatore's wedding begins: 'Looking at the photographs of a wedding taken nearly thirty years ago one can't believe that so many, who now look as they do, once looked like *that*' (*IN* 219). This is a good example of what Frank Kermode called 'the illusion of total specification': if there are photographs, then there was a wedding; if people appear to have changed over time, then someone, the narrator, must be doing the noticing. But who exactly this is remains a mystery.

After writing *Offshore*, Fitzgerald worried that she might not be 'up to [writing] multiple consciousness' novels, yet one of the distinctions of *Innocence*, and *The Gate of Angels* after it, is precisely Fitzgerald's ability to imbue even minor characters with interior lives, and to slip unobtrusively from one character's point of view to another.[9] Two set-piece scenes take us inside Salvatore and Chiara's minds. Aged ten, Salvatore had travelled with his father on a pilgrimage to visit Antonio Gramsci, on his death-bed in Rome. All that Salvatore sees is the grotesqueness of Gramsci's twisted body. He neither knows nor cares about Gramsci's thought and writing, and has no way of understanding his father's devotion to the man and his political ideals. The boy asks Gramsci why he is bleeding:

> as Gramsci opened the other side of his mouth to answer as he had promised, and possibly even to smile, something final and disastrous happened, he leaned forward and dark liquids began to make their escape from several parts of his body. (*IN* 43)

The image of Gramsci's body leaking 'dark liquids' is appalling, yet in Fitzgerald's studied telling ('began to make their escape') it is also darkly cartoonish, and at the same time miraculous, like a cheap plaster statue of a saint weeping or bleeding. Salvatore is shocked into thought and resolves to become a doctor: 'In the end we shall all of us be at the mercy of our own bodies, but at least let me understand what is happening to them' (*IN* 62). A corollary of his commitment to the practical arts is that he becomes witheringly dismissive of those who merely write, make speeches or pose as thinkers: 'the sole task of the intellectual,' he declares, 'is to make people despise what they used to enjoy' (*IN* 69–70). This is Fitzgerald at her roguish best, conveying not only something essential about Salvatore's person, but in his trenchant manner her own distrust of untethered abstraction (witness her satire of the structuralist critic Tite-Live Rochegrosse-Bergson in *The Golden Child*) in contrast to her admiration for practical skills and crafts.

But while Salvatore knows his own mind, Chiara is riven by indecision: 'She knew her tendency to fragment, often against her will, into other existences' (*IN* 82). It is only after years of struggling, and failing, to 'escape from the unsettling vision of other points of view', when Chiara meets Salvatore at a concert in Florence, that she suddenly glimpses another way of living:

> When Salvatore had spoken to her all the distractions had settled, for the first time she could remember since early childhood, into

tranquillity. The relief was indescribable. No more wear and tear of the heart.' (*IN* 83)

The psychological state described here is aptly illustrated by Fitzgerald's note in her working papers about the state of mind of Friedrich von Hardenberg, the protagonist of *The Blue Flower*, when he meets Sophie von Kühn: 'Feeling was not intoxication although "a quarter of an hour decided him", nor calculation. It was just that he felt stability – that is the unity where subjective & objective values are one & there is no clash between inclination & duty.'[10] Fitzgerald applies such fine-grained appreciation of emotional and mental states to numerous characters in *Innocence*. Chiara's father, Count Giancarlo Ridolfi, who 'at the age of sixty-five, had made a serious decision to outface the last part of his life, and indeed of his character, by not minding about anything very much' (*IN* 10) has a presence that belies the relatively small part he has to play in the novel. Giancarlo walks across the fields with his nephew Cesare at the family farm, Valsassina:

> The dog, crouching, followed the sound with sharp attention, hoping that the sound might become a shot. And yet when I was a boy and lived here I was impatient for every morning, the Count thought. (*IN* 26)

In an instant we have slipped from the narrator's point of view to Giancarlo's. 'And yet' seems strange until we realize that it picks up the Count's train of thought, begun a page before, when the Count reflects 'that he was too old for such outings' (*IN* 25). This is extraordinarily deft: the briefest hint of the Count's thinking prompts the reader to imagine the rest of Giancarlo's boyhood at Valsassina, his memories and feelings about the place and the passing years. At the same time, ironically, the Count's musing distracts him from perceiving Cesare's unhappiness at the news of Chiara's impending marriage, or from even beginning to realize why his nephew might feel this way. Such discreet entrances to characters' minds, briefly revealing the complex world of thought and feeling within, while simultaneously acknowledging the selfishness of such interiority, contribute to one of Fitzgerald's most magical effects: the creation of people whose past we feel we know, whose regrets and half-formed ideas resemble our own, and whose future, for this reason, becomes of keen interest to us, extending beyond the world of the novel.

As in all of Fitzgerald's writing, *Innocence* is richly if subtly allusive, evoking a host of half-submerged literary associations. At least four different narrative effects are achieved by these dimly recognized allusions, quotations and echoes: the moulding of particular characters; the production of ironies (for those readers who recognize them); the emanation of a cultural mood belonging to a particular time and place; and a deeper resonance made up of names and phrases, plots and situations, hinting at a profound connection between the events and people of this specific story and more generally applicable human truths. Some allusions function through simple comparison or contrast: Cesare's looks are compared to those of Cesare Pavese; Via Limbo, the address of the Ridolfi's Florentine flat, recalls Dante; and Sannazzaro – a favourite kind of character for Fitzgerald ('a part-time book-keeper, one of those not born to succeed, with the short-sighted mildness of a certain kind of violent revolutionary' (*IN* 46)) – may have had his name from the Italian poet and humanist Jacopo Sannazaro (1458–1530), author of the pastoral poem *Arcadia*. Other instances of intertextuality, such as the three-line inscription on the iron gates of La Ricordanza, contain layers of literary reworking:

> Maggior dolore è ben la Ricordanza –
> senti' dir lor con sì alti sospiri –
> o nell' amaro inferno amena stanza? (*IN* 91)

The first and third lines, which ask if memory ('Ricordanza') is the most wretched of miseries or the one flower of ease in the bitterest hell ('amaro inferno'), are taken verbatim from Dante Gabriel Rossetti's adaptation of Dante's Paulo and Francesca episode in *The Inferno*, 5.121. The second, interpolated line, however, comes word-for-word from Dante's *Purgatorio* 19.74 (translated as 'I heard them say with resounding sighs'). The result is a kind of cento (a poem composed entirely of verses taken from other authors), emblematic both of *Innocence*'s tangential exploration of the present's relationship to the past, and of the novel's complex Italian literary inheritance. The effect is the creation of a wholly authentic fictional time and place, seemingly written from within that world rather than without.

Literary quotations and allusions are also used to reveal aspects of character. Giancarlo, who wishes not to be troubled, quotes from Euripides, *Hippolytus*, ll. 653–61 ('If we could buy children with silver and gold, without women's company! But it cannot be' (*IN* 28)); Barney, with her convent education, paraphrases Romans 3:8 ('It's speaking evil that good may come' (*IN* 122)), and, exhibits her creed of self-reliance by quoting the nineteenth-century Australian poet, jockey and politician, Adam Lindsay Gordon: 'No game was ever yet worth a rap / For a rational man to play, / Into which no accident, no mishap, / Could possibly find its way' (*IN* 282). The love-struck Chiara quotes almost verbatim from Dante's *La Vita Nuova* ('*Amor segnoreggio la anima, la quale fu si tosto a lui disponata*'; 'Love tyrannized over my soul, which was so quickly wedded to him' (*IN* 162)). The novel's wonderfully inconclusive final scene, poised between tragedy and comedy, also alludes, as Hermione Lee observes, to two of Fitzgerald's favourite novels: Ford Madox Ford's *The Good Soldier*, where the narrator Dowell enables Edward Ashburnam to commit suicide, and Turgenev's *Fathers and Sons*, in which Bazarov, like Salvatore, thinks of himself as expendable, 'a superfluous man' (*PF* 321). A Beckettian echo is clearly audible in Salvatore's last words and in Cesare's calm response:

> 'What's to become of us? We can't go on like this.'
> 'Yes, we can go on like this,' said Cesare. 'We can go on exactly like this for the rest of our lives.' (*IN* 339)

But Julian Barnes is right to say that the closing scene is in fact less Beckettian and more Chekhovian 'in the admission that work and life must continue, because that is what has been allotted to us' (*IN* xiv). Never obtrusive, such echoes and allusions combine to produce a literary texture characterized not by opacity but rather by semantic density. And since so many of these allusions are unadvertised but hover just at the edge of perception, the reader of *Innocence* is left with a tangible yet elusive sense of the novel's wider field of reference.

Fascinatingly, Fitzgerald's notebooks contain draft material for a number of other scenes, or possibly a sequel, to *Innocence*. Plans appear to exist for a second part of the story, set more than a decade after the marriage of Chiara and Salvatore. The draft story begins with the arrival in Florence of Matthew Massini, an adviser on private art collections: 'It was raining heavily with a hard silvery persistence and the vineyards, between their rolling stone walls, were as sodden as the Home Counties.'[11] It is a measure of Fitzgerald's achievement in *Innocence* that Chiara, Salvatore, Barney, Giancarlo, Cesare and the other characters are so alive to us that such a small fragment of draft material can hold such allure. Eager to re-enter their world, the reader will have to wait until publication of this draft fragment to do it, but this kind of fully realized time travel is taken, if possible, to even greater heights in Fitzgerald's next novel, *The Beginning of Spring*.

THE BEGINNING OF SPRING (1988)

Fitzgerald worked on *The Beginning of Spring* through 1986 and 1987. The idea for the Russian setting came from her friend, Mary Chamot, whose father had been a businessman in Moscow, selling flowers from his greenhouse before, during and after the 1917 Revolution.[12] The greenhouse disappeared in Fitzgerald's final draft, but she believed that this kind of original image or idea 'always stays so to speak latent, within the novel when it's finished'. The notion of hidden ideas or images in fiction was an important one for Fitzgerald throughout her writing career: 'I can only say that they seem to me close to the mysterious individual life of the novel which you can recognise whether you're reading it or writing it' (*PF* 338).[13] In *The Beginning of Spring*, the image of the greenhouse is replaced by the Reid family's printing works and the tightly defined world of the British merchant community in pre-revolutionary Moscow. The novel is a beautifully realized portrait of Frank Reid's entanglement in this world – by ties of duty, conscience and convention – and of his wish, in part, to escape. Thwarted desire is central to the story, as it is in *Human Voices*, *Innocence*, *The Gate of Angels* and *The Blue Flower*, as both Frank and his wife Nellie come to want more from life than is offered by their marriage.

As ever in Fitzgerald's novels, dilemmas of personal desire are inseparable from larger, more imponderable questions: the nature of truth and kindness, the challenges of communication, and the mysterious relationship between appearance and reality. No one in this Russian world of emotion, irrationality and passion (exemplified by Kuriatin and Volodya) is quite what they seem, and least of all Nellie, Selwyn or Lisa. This was the distinctively Russian mood Fitzgerald had met in books and life. In 1975 she had travelled to Russia, turning the experience into fiction in *The Golden Child*, and, as Hermione Lee observes, 'All her adult life she read Russian novelists, mostly in the Garnett translations, Tolstoy, Dostoevsky, Turgenev, Chekhov, Ostrovosky, Pasternak, Solzhenitsyn' (*PF* 338). Fitzgerald's favourite Russian books were Tolstoy's *Resurrection*, Turgenev's *Fathers and Sons*, the stories of Tatyana Tolstaya, and Andrei Platonov's story 'The Return', translated by Robert Chandler (*PF* 353). For *Punch* in the 1940s, Fitzgerald had reviewed a volume of Russian short stories, identifying the dominant theme of Russian literature as 'pity, limitless pity, extending from the horse standing in the shafts with a broken leg to the soldier on the battle-field and the half-frozen clerk at his desk'. Fitzgerald added that in Tolstoy's *Ivan Ilych* one finds the sentence that is the keynote of the volume: 'His life had been most simple and most ordinary and therefore most terrible.'[14] For Tolstoy, writing after his religious conversion, Ivan Ilych's ordinariness is 'terrible' because his life had been hollow, amoral, without purpose. Fitzgerald took a quite different view. To her, being simple and ordinary was a 'positive condition', like not being wanted, and this quiet conviction, along with the theme of pity, informs her treatment in *The Beginning of Spring* of the seemingly unremarkable couple, Frank and Nellie Reid.[15]

Frank and Nellie's unhappy relationship lies at the heart of the novel. Again and again in her fiction, knowing as Jane Austen knew that this was the oldest and most reliable source of tragicomedy, Fitzgerald depicted the situation of two people not quite fitted to each other, whether because of age, class or both. Frank asks his daughter Dolly whether Nellie did the right thing in leaving. Dolly replies uncompromisingly, 'I don't know whether she did or not. The mistake she probably made was getting married in the first place' (*BS* 62). Nellie Reid (née Cooper) is unlike any other female character in Fitzgerald's fiction. Physically absent for almost the entire novel, Nellie is only known to us indirectly, through Frank's recollections and his brother-in-law Charlie's remarks. Unromantic and practical,

Nellie is largely defined for us by Frank's memories of their courtship, and in particular of her fierce refusal to be done down – 'I'm not going to be got the better of' (*BS* 36) – by the people of Norbury, where she grew up in southwest London. Nellie is far from Fitzgerald's own personality, yet a brief reference to Nellie's miscarriage, like Chiara's in *Innocence*, echoes Fitzgerald's own: 'Nellie lay flat on her back, losing blood, hoping to save the baby. She told Frank to throw some money out of the window to the organ-man to bring them luck, but they had no luck that day' (*BS* 38). Frank is one of Fitzgerald's quiet male heroes, closest to Fred Fairly in *The Gate of Angels*. He is patient and kind but capable of outbursts of feeling, as in his overwhelming desire to make love to Lisa: 'I can only recognize what's solid by touching it, which in this particular case, to be honest, would be by no means enough' (*BS* 118). This capacity for passion in Frank endears him to us, especially by comparison with the stolid, seemingly narrow-minded Nellie. But still, we wonder, what could have prompted her to disappear so suddenly, leaving Frank and her three children behind?

The mysterious world of *The Beginning of Spring* depends for its effects on the minutely observed details of its setting. This is one of the secrets of Fitzgerald's art: her extraordinary distillation, selection and shaping of masses of research. Reidka's printing works springs to life in the mesmeric description of the daily routine of the compositor Tvyordov, as precise and efficient as that of Annie Asra's piano-tuner father in *Human Voices*:

> Tvyordov spent no time in distributing the type from the reserves of the thirty-five letters and fifteen punctuation marks, that had always been done the night before, but started straight away on his copy, memorized the first few phrases, filled his composing stick, adjusted the spaces and took a sounding from his watch to see how long this had taken and to set his standard for the day. (*BS* 48–9)

Fitzgerald's prose itself here, unfolding in a single, multi-clausal sentence, is as methodical, precise and rhapsodically ritualistic as the actions it describes. The typesetter's craft, lovingly described, is rendered all the more real by taking place in the world of events. To that end, political history finds its way into the story through Charlie Cooper's letters from England, telling of mass strikes in 1911, through Frank's discussion with Selwyn of the assassination of the Russian premier, Piotr Stolypin, and through the incorporation into the story of real places, such as the Muir and Merrilees (Muirka's) department store, and real people, such as Tolstoy. Selwyn recounts to Frank his experience of singing at the Korsakov lunatic asylum, of some of the inmates falling asleep, of apologizing to Tolstoy, and of the great man's response: 'I find you have done well. To be bored is the ordinary sensation of most of us at a concert of this kind. But to these unfortunates it is a luxury to have an ordinary sensation' (*BS* 57–8). Fascinatingly, Fitzgerald puts her own sense of the value and dignity of ordinariness here, as something to be aspired to, in the mouth of Tolstoy. In so doing, Tolstoy, like Goethe in *The Blue Flower*, is made all the more real by being revered and gently mocked at the same time. A sense of place is also achieved by an adroit scattering of Russian names, places and words, such as '*podvipevchye* – with just a dear little touch of drunkenness' (*BS* 13). The same effect is achieved with Italian in *Innocence* and German in *The Blue Flower*. Less obviously, but even more memorably, Fitzgerald has a fine ear for the English diction of the era. Before they are married, Nellie asks Frank:

'What were the girls like in Nottingham?'
'I can't remember. Very moderate, I think.' (*BS* 33)

This is deliciously deadpan, like a lower-middle-class version of a line from Noel Coward's *Private Lives*. 'Very moderate' was a common term of depreciation in the Victorian and Edwardian eras, indicating mediocrity; in a typical example of its use, a horse is described as looking 'long in the back' with 'very moderate loins'.[16] But to describe the girls of Nottingham in this way is Frank's gift to Nellie and pure joy for the reader.

For the details of the Russian setting Fitzgerald drew on a number of sources. Principal among them were Harvey Pitcher's *The Smiths of Moscow* (1984), about a family of Scottish boilermakers in Russia before the Revolution, Eugenie Fraser's *The House by the Dvina* (1984), and Ronald Hingley's *Russian Writers and Society 1825–1904* (1967). Fitzgerald's notebooks for the novel are crammed with writing, with sections on Turgenev, on forest and steppe, railways, Frank's biography, the printers' union, Tyvordov and much more.[17] To get some idea of what Moscow was like at the time, Fitzgerald read *The Times* Russian supplements from 1910 to 1913, as well as Baedeker's Russia 1914.[18] Selwyn Crane is an amalgam of Tolstoy's translator and biographer, Aylmer Maude, and Stephen Graham, a British writer and sympathizer with the poor whose books recount his travels around pre-revolutionary Russia.[19] From Pitcher, Fitzgerald borrowed names such as Annushka, Frank, Nellie and Ivanovna, and the description of stoves glazed with tiles from the Vlasov Tile Works.[20] She also adapted, with Pitcher's permission, the story of the bear cub running riot in the dining-room, although Fitzgerald characteristically ups the quotient of violence and cruelty, adding the doorman's panicked scattering of hot coals on the bear, the bear's scream, and young Mitya's brutality: 'When Mitya Kuriatin hit it with a billiard cue it turned its torpedo-shaped head from side to side and then fell over' (*BS* 69). A typical example of Fitzgerald's reworking of her source material comes at the beginning of Chapter 2:

> Up till a few years ago the first sound in the morning in Moscow had been the cows coming out of the side-streets where they were kept in stalls and backyards, and making their own way among the horse-trams to their meeting point at the edge of the Khamovniki, where they were taken by the municipal cowman to their pasture, or, in winter, through the darkness, to the suburban stores of hay. Since the tram-lines were electrified, the cows had disappeared. (*BS* 12)

This conflates a speech and a passage of description in *The Smiths of Moscow*:

> 'In the early morning these cows are let out, and make their way to a barrier of the city; others join, and when they all arrive, there are a goodly number; at the barrier they meet a man with a horn, who drives them in a body to pasture, and collects them again in the evening, when they all return independently each to her own stable.'

> Moscow was changing rapidly. The old horse-drawn trams were being replaced by electric ones, although they still used kerosene lamps in the house, and the Works still relied on its own generators. No longer were the cows driven along Smith Street every morning to their pasture in the Testov Field beyond the Smith Lake.[21]

The principal difference between Fitzgerald's description and those of her sources is the rhythm of the prose. Fitzgerald's account is distinguished by its imitative harmony, using one long sentence to insinuate the movement of the cows meandering to the pastures and back, then one short one, mourning the demise of the ritual caused by the electrification of the trams. Fitzgerald also changes the tense of her source, from present and imperfect in *The Smiths of Moscow* to pluperfect in *The Beginning of Spring*. Fitzgerald's version ('Since the tramlines were electrified, the cows had disappeared') is what a Muscovite would say, with regret for the passing of a treasured custom. By such means Fitzgerald's narrative gives the oft-noted impression of having been written from *inside* the fictional world and culture of the novel. 'To excavate these sources is not to diminish Fitzgerald's imaginative brilliance,' as Hermione Lee observes, 'but, on the contrary, to show how, while using them closely and freely, she gives the appearance of having done no homework at all, and makes her fictive world seem real' (*PF* 346). One glance at Fitzgerald's notebooks, brimful with writing, reveals the sheer volume of research so deftly worked into the grain of the novel that it becomes invisible.

Similarly, literary echoes, allusions and evocations, some barely detectable, deepen the layers of feeling and pathos and imbue the novel with its distinctively enigmatic atmosphere of unpredictability. As Frank flees from Miss Kinsman through the back alleys of Moscow, the dingy shops themselves seem to speak: 'Bring me your broken shoes, your worn-out mattresses, your legless chairs, your headless beds, and in some basement workshop or hole in the wall I will make them serviceable, at least for a few months or so' (*BS* 88), echoing Emma Lazarus's famous sonnet on the Statue of Liberty: 'Give me your tired, your poor, / Your huddled masses yearning to breathe free.' The effect of the parallel is not to diminish Lazarus's poem, but to ennoble the humble repair shops of Kolbasov Pereulok (Kolbasov Lane). The pre-revolutionary period is evoked through references to J. M. Barrie's *Peter Pan*, still hugely popular in 1913, and fiction read by Uncle Charlie such as *Sentimental Tommy* (also by Barrie) and E. W. Hornung's *Raffles* short stories, and to Tolstoy's *Resurrection* and Jerome K. Jerome's *Three Men in a Boat*. Such instances make up the visible surface of overt quotation and reference in *The Beginning of Spring*. However, moments of comedy in the novel also contain a largely *invisible* substrate of literary allusion. For example, Romantic, idealist thought in *The Beginning of Spring*, usually voiced by Selwyn Crane, is gently mocked. Frank asks Selwyn whether he considers him to be unkind. Selwyn replies:

'That, Frank, must be a question of the imagination, I mean of picturing the sufferings of others. Now, you're not an imaginative man, Frank. If you have a fault, it's that you don't grasp the importance of what is beyond sense or reason. And yet that is a world in itself. "Where is the stream," we cry, with tears. But look up, and lo! there is the blue stream flowing gently over our heads.' (*BS* 202)

Hermione Lee mentions that Selwyn's speech is an unattributed quotation from *Heinrich von Ofterdingen*, by the German Romantic poet Novalis, the subject of *The Blue Flower* (*PF* 390). But the literary echoes do not end there. This precise quotation is the epigraph to Chapter 2 of George Macdonald's fantasy novel *Phantastes* (1858), which Fitzgerald loved. Indeed it was her fondness for Macdonald that led Fitzgerald to Novalis in the first place.[22] Fitzgerald makes affectionate fun of Selwyn's effusions in part to gives us Frank's more rational and practical point of view. Yet at the same time, brilliantly and seemingly paradoxically, the effect of such teasing is in fact to make her reader more receptive to high-flown ideas and images.

The air of mystery and ambiguity created by Fitzgerald in *The Beginning of Spring* is unmatched in her writing, with the possible exception of *The Blue Flower*. The notion of a world beyond sight is evoked by Fitzgerald's characteristic interest in metaphysics: 'The store keeper had told him that, in his opinion, soul and body were like the steam above a factory, one couldn't exist without the other' (*BS* 154). More mundanely, tiny hints are dropped about Selwyn, Nellie and Lisa. We know that *something* is amiss, but, like Frank, we struggle to piece it together: 'He had the impression that they were avoiding an important aspect of the subject, but felt too tired to work out what it was' (*BS* 102–3). Selwyn is at the heart of the plot, the build up to his revelation of his failed tryst with Nellie proceeds by hints and indirection. Selwyn says that he wants 'a serious talk' with Frank; later, Selwyn seems 'exceptionally pale'. Yet when his admission comes, the reader is as surprised as Frank to hear that, 'Nellie saw me in a false glow, my friend' (*BS* 236). This at least explains why Nellie left in the first place, intending to go away with Selwyn to 'some more free and natural place' (*BS* 237). But some questions remain unanswered: what is Selwyn's connection to Lisa? He mentions to Frank that: 'She has had some education, at one time they wanted to make a teacher of her' (*BS* 100), but who or what are '*they*'? Is it significant that the police know Selwyn (*BS* 144), and is there collusion between them? Is that why he places Lisa, who perhaps is suspected as a Bolshevik, with Frank, so that she can be observed? Lisa herself is a figure of even greater mystery and remains so to Frank: 'She seemed, however, as always, to be listening only enough to grasp what was said and to respond to it correctly and efficiently, while compelled to hear, by some inner secret conspiracy, another voice' (*BS* 217). The mention of 'secret conspiracy' hints at Lisa's revolutionary affiliation, and later, when Lisa disappears, apparently to Berlin, Frank finally begins to understand recent events, why the Security was in favour of him leaving Russia. 'He had dangerous employees, or one dangerous employee, at least, a dangerous young woman, pretending to be looking after his children. He had let her escape, more likely arranged it' (*BS* 243). Earlier, Frank had given Lisa back her papers without reporting it to the authorities (*BS* 161). But who, Frank wonders, could have known this, and who might have suggested it to the Security? Though we might suspect Selwyn, we are left, like Frank, without a clear answer.

Such mysteries of plot, of politics and even of metaphysics come together in one of the most powerful scenes in the novel, Lisa and Dolly in the forest at Shirokaya. 'On the third night, Dolly woke, and knew she had been woken, by the slight noise of a door opening, the door on the veranda. The noise did not strike her as frightening, rather as something she had been expecting' (*BS* 227). Dolly finds Lisa on the veranda and asks her where she is going. Lisa replies: 'It might have been better if you hadn't woken up, but you did wake up. Now you'll have to come with me' (*BS* 227). Dolly follows Lisa through the forest, through 'the plunging half-darkness':

> Then Dolly began to see on each side of her, among the thronging stems of the birch trees, what looked like human hands, moving to touch each other across the whiteness and blackness.

'Lisa,' she called out, 'I can see hands.'
Lisa stood still again. They were in a clearing into which the moon shone. Dolly saw that by every birch tree, close against the trunk, stood a man or a woman. They stood separately pressing themselves each to their own tree. Then they turned their faces towards Lisa, patches of white against the whiteish bark. Dolly saw that there were many more of them, deep into the thickness of the wood. (*BS* 228–9)

Who are these wraith-like figures? Revolutionaries? Dryadic spirits of the Russian birch? Figments of Dolly's dream? Fascinatingly, we find a prefiguring of this scene in a *World Review* editorial of 1950, co-signed by Fitzgerald and Desmond, describing Barcelona's Parque Güell: 'As you go higher, it gets darker, and you find, by putting out your hand, that you can no longer tell the difference between the trees and stone columns made like trees, or faces and half-human shapes growing out of the walls.'[23] Fitzgerald's own working notes also offer a clue to her intentions: 'Lisa to impress upon Dolly that she's seen people who are prepared to give their lives serious. not too much'.[24] Fitzgerald's replacement of 'prepared to give their lives' with 'serious', and the underlined imperative to herself, are crucial. Restraint is the watchword, less being so much more.

'I have come, but I can't stay,' said Lisa. 'You came, all of you, as far as this on my account. I know that, but I can't stay. As you see, I've had to bring this child with me. If she speaks about this, she won't be believed. If she remembers it, she'll understand in time what she's seen.'
No one answered her, no one spoke. No one left the protection of the trees, or moved towards them. (*BS* 229)

The echo here of Fitzgerald's favourite poet, Walter de la Mare, the master of the nocturnal, is unmistakeable: 'Tell them I came, and no one answered / That I kept my word' ('The Listeners', ll. 1–2). We guess now that Lisa is indeed the leader of some kind of political group. But, told from Dolly's drowsy perspective, and shrouded in darkness and shadow, the scene, like the book as a whole, leaves sufficient room for doubt and imagination as each reader, in Fitzgerald's words, seeks to recognize 'the mysterious individual life of the novel'.

THE GATE OF ANGELS (1990)

Like *The Bookshop*, *The Gate of Angels* begins with a clearly signalled presage of upheavals to come. In the fields outside Cambridge cows wallow helplessly among uprooted willows: 'A scene of disorder, tree-tops on the earth, legs in the air, in a university city devoted to logic and reason' (*GA* 3). Set in 1912 in the early years of particle physics, Fitzgerald's third novel on a historical theme fizzes with the ideas and disputes of the day: the nature of the atom, women's right to vote, and whether science has done away with the soul. But the opening image serves as a warning that in this novel anything and everything might happen – and it does. The unstoppable natural force that tears up logic and reason in *The Gate of Angels* is love at first sight. Fred Fairly is a country rector's son, lecturer in physics and Junior Fellow at the college of St Angelicus. Daisy Saunders, brought up in hard-scrabble South London, is a nurse probationer at Blackfriars Hospital. Fred and Daisy's lives converge when their bicycles collide and they wake to find themselves together in bed.[25] 'My God, what luck,' thinks Fred (*GA* 63). Divided by class, education and upbringing, Fred and Daisy's relationship forms the movement of the novel. 'The movement should be what readers want to happen,' Fitzgerald wrote. 'You should hope, if you read this book, that Fred and Daisy would end up happily'.[26] The reader's wish for a happy ending for hero and heroine in *The Gate of Angels*, more than in any other Fitzgerald work, is one of two lasting impressions peculiar to this novel. The other is the powerful and occasionally disturbing sense that another, more unfathomable story lies beneath the tale we are reading. How are these two impressions achieved?

Readers care so much about Fred and Daisy because, uniquely among the odd couples in Fitzgerald's novels, they are evenly matched. Both are highly intelligent (in different ways), young, kind-hearted and uncomplaining. Having seen Daisy just once, Fred falls deeply and utterly in love: 'there is no purpose in the universe, but if there were, it could be shown that there was an intention, throughout recorded and unrecorded time, to give me Daisy' (*GA* 133). Miraculously, Daisy seems worthy of such devotion: instinctively generous, brave and clear-eyed about human weakness, including her own. Told by the matron at Blackfriars that women must expect to spend a quarter of their lives in pain, 'Daisy felt a rush of admiration. So far she herself had done nothing like her fair share' (*GA* 90). 'Daisy is a fearless survivor,' Fitzgerald observed, 'a favourite type with the late-Victorian and Edwardian light novelists' (*HA* 513). But Daisy's instinct to give rather than take is also her undoing. Worn down by defeat after losing her job, Daisy lets the predatory newspaper editor Thomas Kelly accompany her to Cambridge. 'He put his arm round her waist, fingering her. What a pair we make, she thought. He doesn't deserve any better, no more do I' (*GA* 128). There is no sadder line in Fitzgerald's writing. When the truth finally emerges, that Kelly had booked a room at Pett's Hotel in Cambridge for him and Daisy, the chaos promised by the cows cavorting among the willows finally breaks out. Daisy and Fred part without a word, then quarrel and part again, seemingly irreconcilable.

At the heart of this quarrel, and of the novel, are conflicting attitudes to truth. For Fred the scientist, nothing is more important. In the court case about the cycling accident, Daisy denies knowing Kelly. Later Fred silently implores her to say that she lied to spare his, Fred's, feelings. 'Say it, Daisy, say it, say it.' But she doesn't. 'Of course I don't tell lies unless I've got to', she retorts defensively, stung by his questions (*GA* 205). But is even this true? In a seemingly trivial moment on their walk in the country, Daisy admitted to making up the name of a flower, a throatwort, explaining, 'I only said it to keep things going' (*GA* 147). Fitzgerald's notebooks for *The Gate of Angels* reveal the centrality of honesty to her thinking: 'Daisy to marry Editor, because both are liars...the bonds between liars, as against truth-tellers are as strong as agnostics v. faithful.'[27] Yet in the writing of the novel, something clearly changed. (The manuscript of *The Gate of Angels* is as heavily worked as those of any of her novels.) The concept of truth in *The Gate of Angels* becomes less absolute and more conditional. In plain economic terms the truth is shown to be more affordable for some than for others. Daisy admonishes Fred for knocking Kelly down: 'His job's nothing to be proud of, but then he didn't have your advantages. You think of that the next time you come across a poor sod like Kelly' (*GA* 206). As Fred comes to realize, truth and honesty are not necessarily the paramount virtues. More important still is kindness, the instinct to help that loses Daisy her job but which, on the very last page, magically wins her and Fred a chance of happiness.

The reader's sympathy for Fred and Daisy is also elicited by their shared understanding of ordinary human weakness, the latter brilliantly realized by Fitzgerald in an array of memorable minor characters. Daisy understands why Kelly behaves as he does, even if she doesn't condone it, and she pities rather than condemns the conniving Mrs Martinez, who explains to Daisy why she tapped her for money: 'I didn't ask you for it because I was poor. I asked because you never forget anyone who borrows money from you and I don't want you to forget me' (*GA* 124). This is perversely but inescapably logical. The novel affords us many such glimpses of the way minds work, surrounding Fred and Dairy with a believably oddball collection of family, friends and enemies with whom they must coexist. Holcombe, a demonstrator at the new chemistry labs, is a blundering monomaniac, oblivious to everything but his own train of thought: 'When Fred next met him, he would start straight away from where his letter had broken off, as though between words spoken and words written there was no dividing line' (*GA* 13). That Fred puts up with Holcombe when he could just as easily not is a sign of his good nature. Other relationships are matters of duty rather than choice. The Provost of St James's, the medievalist and palaeographer Dr Matthews (a thinly disguised M. R. James), is supremely feline, seemingly amiable yet watchful and faintly sinister, waiting for his moment to pounce:

> 'You're coming in, I hope, for that pipe?'
> Fred said he was afraid he didn't smoke.
> 'You mean, of course, that you do,' said the Provost, stroking his cat triumphantly. (*GA* 60)

We sense, even in this briefest of exchanges, that something is eluding our grasp. It may well be, simply, that the Provost can't conceive of a man not smoking. Much later in the novel Dr Matthews muses to himself, incredulously: 'I met a man lately, a scientist, who had never smoked a pipe' (*GA* 164). But at this earlier point in the story, *this* is all we have to go on, making us suspect hidden meanings. The feeling arises in part precisely as an effect of the extreme brevity of the scene, of what has been called the novel's remarkable 'density of implication'. As Frank Kermode noted, in *The Gate of Angels* 'one senses a developed interest in the mysteriousness of the story, the exploitation of a new skill, which is to arrange for the story to project another story, less definite, more puzzling, than the first-hand narrative itself'.[28] It is through intimating that another richer, more profound story lies behind the apparently hapless collisions and quarrels of poor Fred and Daisy that the book exerts its strange power.

This sense of the untold story, of something at the edge of our perception, is everywhere in the novel. In the seemingly bucolic peace of Blow: 'Twigs snapped and dropped from above, sticky threads drifted across from nowhere, there seemed to be something like an assassination, on a small scale, taking place in the tranquil heart of summer' (*GA* 40–1). The idea of sinister goings-on in unsuspected places produces a ripple of unease in the reader. Disquiet is later converted into a more recognizably and overt Gothic atmosphere in Fitzgerald's wonderfully macabre pastiche of an M. R. James ghost story. Read by Dr Matthews to Hartley, the Junior Dean of James's, the gruesome tale of insane nuns who stuff a man into a culvert then suck the flesh off his body bears an oddly skewed parallel to the story of Fred and Daisy and the missing cyclist and carter. 'We shall have to proceed, you see, by analogy,' Dr Matthews says to himself, 'which is a less respectable method than it used to be with theologians, but more respectable, I am told, with scientists' (*GA* 164). Nothing is spelled out and the reader who begs for simple explanations is 'merely waved on with a smile'.[29] But we sense that there *is* a connection between the tale of Fred and Daisy and the story-within-a-story, if only we could figure out what it was. Fitzgerald's shifting narrative point-of-view contributes to the reader's sense that the parallel, however uncertain, may nonetheless be real. The third person narration ('Dr Matthews had been pondering over Fred's accident'), glides inside Matthews's mind as he makes a series of notes: 'One would assume that....If we want to find a man....I return to the carter....I believe, after all, that the best way to the truth may be to tell you a story' (*GA* 163–4). The narration carries the reader fluidly from exterior to interior, but crucially we are not asked to believe in the supernatural any more than Matthews does himself: 'I have been asked, not once, but often, do I believe these things? Well, I can only say that I am prepared to consider the evidence, and accept it if I am satisfied' (*GA* 176). Fitzgerald asks no more and no less of the reader of her novel.

Even more conducive to the dimly felt sense of another story behind this one, are the isolated moments where the narrator unexpectedly intrudes on the reader's consciousness. After the trial, Fred waits in a café for Kelly to emerge:

> He ordered a cup of tea and two biscuits for five pence and thought of nothing. – Oh, but that's impossible. – It's not possible to think of nothing. Certainly it was unprofessional of Fred, who was paid by the university to use his mind, and unwise of him as a lover, but there it was, he was occupied with bitter sensations, giving way to stupefaction, then to emptiness. (*GA* 188)

Whose voice is it that interjects here? At first we think it is Fred's, but it can't be. It must be the narrator suddenly breaking off to challenge his or her own words. The effect is stunning: like a figure appearing through a wall with no doorway, the narrator's interruption gives the reader the briefest, almost subliminal, glimpse of a larger, baffling reality. It is Fitzgerald's remarkable achievement that the reader's imaginative involvement in the telling of the story is not reduced or compromised by the narrative intrusion but only deepened and enlarged by it.

Deftly embedded allusions to the books, poems and hymns of the period play their part in securing the reader's involvement in the novel's time, place and characterization. Brief mentions of Arthur Sullivan's comic opera *Cox and Box* and Rupert Brooke as Mephistopheles in 'the second production of the Marlowe Society's *Doctor Faustus*' (*GA* 155) evoke cultural life in Cambridge in 1912. As a Sunday choirboy, Fred had sung, 'Teach me to live, that I may dread / The grave as little as my bed', from the hymn by Thomas Tallis and Thomas Ken (*GA* 37); the Fairly family dogs are named after a bestselling children's book, Thomas Day's *The History of Sandford and Merton* (1783–9); and when Fred's family visits Cambridge, his sister Julia quotes two lines from 'Young and Old', a poem from the hugely popular *Water Babies* (1862–3) by Charles Kingsley: 'We said God grant you find some face, lad, you knew when all was young' (*GA*

156).[30] Such snatches of poetry, hymns and pet names provide an acute sense of Fred's rectory childhood. Fred himself, in turning away from religion, borrows words from William James's *The Varieties of Religious Experience* (1901–2) that come close to expressing his despair: 'We should have spoken earlier, prayed for another world absolutely, before this world was born' (*GA* 55). We are told little or none of this. Fitzgerald's silent working of her sources into the foundations of her novels is at the heart of her writing. Books that she read on the urban poor, like George Gissing's *The Nether World* (1889), on nursing, such as Eva Luckes's *Hospital Sisters and their Duties* (1912), and Edwardian comic novels such as the Grossmiths' *Diary of a Nobody* (1888–9), Barry Pain's *Eliza* (1900) or the novels of W. W. Jacobs, all inform and shape, in different ways and degrees, the authentic Edwardian air breathed by *The Gate of Angels*. The affection with which Fitzgerald portrays Cambridge also owes something to the fact that this was the world of her Uncle Dillwyn, which she had recreated in *The Knox Brothers*. The Disobligers' Society gets its name from one of Dillwyn's absurd college debating groups, 'The As It Were In Contradistinction Society' (*PF* 368), and Fred's loss of belief recalls Dilly's abandoning of his faith. As Fitzgerald continued to move further away from autobiography, here and in her final novel, *The Blue Flower*, allusion becomes the chief means by which the people, place and mood of the novel are infused with personal and deeply held memories and feelings.

By Fitzgerald's own admission, *The Gate of Angels* is the only one of her novels with a happy ending. When the slight delay caused by Daisy's detour into St Angelicus causes her to meet Fred walking slowly home, it's hard not to shout with joy. Our hero and heroine finding each other casts a glow on our own dreams of happiness: 'Evidently he meant it and Daisy perceived at that moment that what he was offering her was the best of himself, keeping nothing back, the best, then, that one human being can offer to another' (*GA* 150). The reader takes pleasure too in the comic restoration of order: the cows and the trees have been righted and reason and logic have their place, now in balance with kindness and understanding. Fitzgerald's vision in *The Gate of Angels*, like Jean Renoir's in *La Règle du Jeu* (1939), is to understand all and judge nothing. Daisy accepts the treachery of Mrs Martinez, Kelly's informer at Blackfriars, in this spirit: 'I suppose there's someone who wants to earn a bit extra there, like all the rest of us' (*GA* 126). Everyone has her reasons. Remarkably, Fitzgerald keeps all of this in play in a novel that is also about the relative merits of truth and compassion, the observable and invisible, natural and supernatural, and as Fitzgerald has it, body, mind and spirit. It is indisputably mysterious in what is not said, yet at the same time briskly impatient even with the notion of mystery: 'Mystery is a luxury and would have been quite beyond her [Daisy's] means' (*GA* 136). Shortlisted for the Booker Prize in 1990, along with novels by Beryl Bainbridge, John McGahern, Brian Moore and Mordechai Richler, *The Gate of Angels* lost out to A. S. Byatt's *Possession*. The miracle of *The Gate of Angels* is that it covers as much if not more emotional, spiritual and intellectual ground than the brilliant *Possession*, but in less than half the distance.

THE BLUE FLOWER (1995)

Penelope Fitzgerald's final and most ambitious novel brings the biographer's and novelist's art together. Set in pre-Napoleonic Saxony, the novel recounts the early years of the German Romantic poet Georg Friedrich ('Fritz') von Hardenberg (1772–1801), better known as 'Novalis' (derived from an old family name, meaning 'clearer of new land'), author of *Hymns to the Night* (*Hymnen an die Nacht*). The novel tells the story of Fritz's improbable love affair, at the age of twenty-six, with the twelve-year-old Sophie von Kühn. Like *The Gate of Angels*, *The Blue Flower* is a novel as much about matter and spirit as it is about love, but it is powerfully about this too. Fitzgerald came to Novalis partly through reading D. H. Lawrence's novella *The Fox* (1922), which refers to the 'fatal flower of happiness, which trembles so blue and lovely in a crevice just beyond your grasp'.[31] Lawrence's 'fatal flower' is itself an allusion to the mysterious blue flower dreamt of in Novalis's unfinished *Bildungsroman*, *Heinrich von Ofterdingen*. Fritz tells the beginning of this story on three separate occasions in *The Blue Flower*. Novalis and his story of the blue flower, identified by Fitzgerald as the Alpine blue gentian, was a well-known subject in Europe when Fitzgerald wrote the novel, but far less so in Britain. Fitzgerald commented that she 'always wondered how DHL knew it was blue, and never quite managed to find out all I wanted to, partly because Novalis' letters to Sophie have disappeared, buried in her grave I daresay' (*SI* 453). Drawn to the mystery of the story and the idea of a quest, Fitzgerald had also always been fascinated by the powerful symbolism of flowers.[32]

Written in fragments and vignettes, in the manner of the German Romantics, the style of *The Blue Flower* accommodates itself to its enigmatic subject. Everything is condensed yet minutely precise. What is left unsaid or unexplained only further evokes, in such a short novel, an entire world of the senses, emotions and ideas. Characters such as Fritz and Sophie seem to step out of the pages and transcend their historical moment: 'the curve of the back and the swing of the coat so familiar as to imply that they should be permanent fixtures in the world, when in fact nothing is more perishable'.[33] The corollary of this condition of perishability is tragicomic longing, for kindness, contentment, glimpses of the numinous, for reunion, with the living and dead. Such varieties of longing are the keynote of *The Blue Flower*. The means by which this note is sounded – narrative density, subtle shifts in point of view, syntax, diction and prose rhythm that signal translation from an alien culture, a myth or symbol central to the novel, extremely precise specification, unattributed quotations and allusions, pervasive comic irony – is the focus of what follows.

The concentrated narrative style of *The Blue Flower* strikes its reader immediately. Fritz's friend, Jacob Dietmahler, who arrives at the Hardenberg family home on washday, understands that the 'great dingy snowfalls' of linen, shirts and underclothes might not mean wealth, 'but it was certainly an indication of long standing' (*BF* 1). Every image, speech and scene works like this to draw the reader's attention not only to the surface of things, but beneath the surface, to what it *feels* like to inhabit this lost world. For students such as Fritz and Dietmahler, who had thrilled at Jena to Fichte's lectures on ideas and the mind, the sheer excitement of living can hardly be contained:

'Fritz, how many are there in your family?' asked Dietmahler. 'So many things?' Then he shouted suddenly: 'There is no such concept as a thing in itself!' (*BF* 2)

Such eruptions, revealing hidden depths of thought and feeling, surge up under the pressure of narrative compression. Sudden glimpses of a symbolic or philosophical dimension, shadowing the primary story, owe much to the fantastical, parabolic, folk story narrative style of George Macdonald's *Phantastes* (1858). Hints in Fitzgerald's later fictions at a world beyond this one led A. S. Byatt to conclude that Fitzgerald's novels are best approached as 'very English versions of European metaphysical fables, embodying them in idiosyncratic reality' (*SI* xiii). But sometimes the sudden outburst has nothing metaphysical about it at all. Fritz's mother reveals that due to the cold she has not undressed at night, even in summer, for twelve years. '"And yet you've given birth to eight of us!" cried Sidonie. "God in heaven spare me a marriage like yours!"' (*BF* 5). At other times the story's fabular quality gives way easily to unexpectedly poignant moments. Sophie's grown-up sister, known by everyone as 'The Mandelsloh', tells a story to her younger siblings of a man who died because he felt no pain, and so had no warning that he was ill:

> 'We don't want any warnings,' the children told her. 'We get into enough trouble as it is.'
> 'But he had no time to consider how he had spent his life, and to repent.'
> 'Repentance is for old women and arse-holes,' shouted George.
> 'George, no-one can tolerate you,' said Frederike. 'They ought to whip you at school.'
> 'They do whip me at school,' said George. (*BF* 175)

Children and adults talking at cross purposes produce the darkly comic pathos of the scene's ending, but a tiny, barely noticeable detail also heightens what Byatt refers to as the scene's 'idiosyncratic reality'. By switching in the middle of the scene from one version of The Mandelsloh's name to another ('Frederike'), Fitzgerald subtly brings us closer to George's rueful point of view, reminding us that The Mandelsloh is George's sister, and that 'Frederike' is what *he* would have called her.

The Blue Flower also contains an unexpected moment in narration that would not be out of place in contemporary experimental fiction:

> Anton nodded, and continued with a setting of some of Zinzendorf's hymns for the Brethren, passing on to the airs from two or three Singspiele and the, what was the piece he played after that? – that very beautiful piece, I did not know it, could Anton have improvised it himself? (*BF* 219)

The almost imperceptible move from the third to the first person here – 'that very beautiful piece, I did not know it' – shakes us from our absorption in Anton's playing, as though someone had spoken. Yet the moment is so fleeting, just a brief flicker, like *déjà-vu* or a dream, that one might hardly notice. 'The tune Anton plays, which no one can quite name, is like the story of the blue flower. It is something you seem always to be on the edge of remembering or identifying. And it runs through the novel like a recurrent tune' (*PF* 405). But who is the 'I' of 'I did not know it'? It can hardly be any of the other characters present. It must belong to the narrator, who from this moment on we see differently, as someone who belongs to the very story he or she is telling. But still, we can only guess. 'She has the gift of knowing, or seeming to know, everything necessary, and as it were knowing it from the inside, conveying it by gleams and fractions, leaving those who feel so disposed to make it explicit.'[34] By such gleams and fractions Fitzgerald gradually builds up a subtle but powerful sense of a semi-permeable division between author and story, past and present, body and spirit.

The Blue Flower, like *Innocence* and *The Beginning of Spring*, also exerts fascination through an alluring foreignness, and in this case there are no English characters to mediate or interpret events. The setting among the Moravian Brotherhood is an unworldly world unto itself. Dialogue is a simulacrum of period German – '"Linnets! They won't go far!" shouted George. "Three at a time I could crunch them"' (*BF* 101) – where the secret is syntax and vocabulary. The sequence of object-subject-verb signals that this is an English approximation of George's German. The physical world itself is luminously animate:

> The sun was down, only the upper sky glowed. The mist was walking up the water. The little boy was not at the ferry. A few pigs

and a flock of geese, forbidden to go by way of Weissenfels' handsome bridge, were waiting for the last crossing. (*BF* 14)

Is this the world as Fritz sees it: a spiritualized version of Goethe's popular ballad *Der Zauberlehrling* ('The Sorcerer's Apprentice'), in which all things – the mist, the pigs, the geese – are somehow conscious, imbued with a human sense of duty and destiny? Or, to be more precise, since the description is told in the third person, is this the world as the unidentified narrator sees it, as a participant in events rather than merely an omniscient yet remote overseer? Again, we can only guess, immersed as deeply as we are in both the physical and mental world of the story.

A crucial source and inspiration for Fitzgerald's evocation of that world is the peculiar atmosphere of Novalis's own writing. 'Poetry, prose, and philosophy are so closely related in Novalis's *oeuvre* – and Fitzgerald shifts so easily between them in the *Blue Flower* – that they emerge as aspects of the same discourse, one that scans, not without a tinge of irony, what the imagination summons into existence.'[35] Nowhere is this scanning or searching more brilliantly realized than in Fritz's vision in the churchyard in Weissenfels, derived from Novalis's *Blüthenstaub* (*Pollen*):[36]

> The creak and thump of the pastor's cows could still be heard far into the burial ground where the graves and the still empty spaces, cut off from each other now by the mist, had become dark green islands, dark green chambers of meditation. On one of them, just a little ahead of him, a young man, still almost a boy, was standing in the half darkness, with his head bent, himself as white, still, and speechless as a memorial. The sight was consoling to Fritz, who knew that the young man, although living, was not human, but also that at the moment that there was no boundary between them. (*BF* 156)

The muted lyricism of this, in which even the hint of transcendence is rendered in the most everyday language, comes close to the rhythms and repetitions of poetry. The 'dark green chambers of meditation' evoke Andrew Marvell's 'all that's made' ('The Garden') and the philosophical reflection elicited from Fritz – 'The universe, after all, is within us' – reverberates through the novel, reappearing just a few pages later in the wonderfully mundane domesticity of Kreisamtmann

Just's happy dissatisfaction with the exact placing of the *Vorbau*, or porch, to his garden-house: 'he would never be quite satisfied with it, never cease to build and rebuild it in his mind. The universe, after all, is within us' (*BF* 167). Poetry, prose and philosophy are melded here in a way characteristic of this novel. At the heart of the story is the mystery of the blue flower itself. The flower is a symbol embodying an untranslatable concept of German Romanticism, 'Sehnsucht', a yearning which cannot be defined or fulfilled, but which is something like nostalgia or homesickness (*PF* 396). Several different interpretations are offered of Fritz's story of the blue flower. The perceptive Mandelsloh, parted from her husband, comes close to its emotional heart: 'He looks for another dear head on the pillow' (*BF* 140). Karoline Just, suffering in silence, only knows what the blue flower is *not*, poetry or happiness. The doctor, Hoftrat Ebhard, 'had never had the chance to hear the opening of *The Blue Flower*, but if he had done so he could have said immediately what he thought it meant': an emblem of tuberculosis, of which 'one in four of his patients died' (*BF* 172–3). The youngest von Hardenberg, the precocious Bernhard, lying in bed at Schlöben, draws his own conclusions:

> He had been struck... by one thing in particular: the stranger who had spoken at the dinner table about the Blue Flower and been understood by one person and one only. This person must have been singled out as distinct from all the rest of the family. It was a matter of recognising your own fate and greeting it as familiar when it came. (*BF* 250)

The Bernhard's understanding becomes especially poignant when, later, we learn how he drowns in the Saale. This method, inducing us to cast our minds back to the significance of earlier hints and moments in the light of later events, is characteristic of Fitzgerald's late style. But what is evident from these different readings, by The Mandelsloh, Karoline, Ebhard and The Bernhard, is that each person interprets the story according to what matters most to them. The blue flower, then, means something different with each telling: mortality or immortality, a universal language, love or fate. Fitzgerald's own notes say candidly about the meaning of the blue flower: 'It might be something you once knew & have forgotten or something you've given up as impossible but in any case your solution is just as good as mine.'[37] For Fritz himself, the fragment of the story about the blue flower appears to hold a talismanic significance, perhaps because of rather than in spite of its resistance to easy interpretation.

As in all of her later novels, Fitzgerald's compositional method was to read everything remotely relevant, then leave almost all of it out. A blue notebook in Fitzgerald's working papers contains an intimidating mass of reading and notes to do with life in the 1790s, concerning people (magistrates, Moravians, doctors, teachers and servants), places (Saxony, Jena, Weimar), things (rings, horses, pianos, food), events (war, politics), ideas (philosophy, religion, science), drawing on, among things, Coleridge's notebooks, Novalis's diaries and books on saltworks, botany and a history of monarchies.[38] A letter written to Fitzgerald in 1992, about salt production and salt-works from a saltmine museum in Halle, was signed by the director, 'Just'. A descendant, perhaps, Fitzgerald must have wondered, of Fritz's friend and supervisor, August Coelestin Just?[39] Fitzgerald's art is to find the gold in the washes, extracting the essence of her reading and displaying infinite care in the selection and shaping of her material, what Candia McWilliam calls Fitzgerald's method of 'knitting up' (*BF* xiii). In this process, priority is always given to imaginative rather than factual reality. 'I ought perhaps to have made it clear,' Fitzgerald wrote to her German translator, 'that this is an interpretation, not an accurate account'.[40] Literary echoes, allusions and quotations enrich this imaginative reality. Quotations from Novalis himself, in English translation, establish the book's Romantic and philosophical spirit, not least *The Blue Flower*'s epigraph, 'Novels arise out of the shortcoming of history' (taken from *Fragmente und Studien*, 1799–1800). More glancing allusions draw on sources far beyond the time and place of the story. Fritz's brother Erasmus says that he is nothing 'but an encumberer of the ground' (*BF* 265), echoing Michael Henchard's abject cry in Hardy's *Mayor of Casterbridge*: 'I, an outcast, an encumberer of the ground, wanted by nobody, and despised by all, live on against my will!' Such strictly literary reverberations (Hardy wrote his novel almost a century after Erasmus von Hardenburg died) tell us about Erasmus, the pitch of his feeling and the kind of imagination he possesses, while also gesturing at something larger, going beyond the world of this particular story, felt by us all. In such a novel of ideas, tone is everything. Throughout the book Fitzgerald's wit reliably and amusingly punctures intellectual pomposity: 'Fichte was speaking of the philosophy of Kant, which, fortunately,' the narrator reports deadpan, 'he had been able to improve upon greatly' (*BF* 37). Hermione Lee points out that debunking romantic fervour with mundane interventions is an old strategy: Byron did it in *Don Juan*, Flaubert in *Madame Bovary* (*PF* 403). Yet Fitzgerald dares to use the technique not just against the pretensions of obvious targets, but against her own hero, Fritz himself. Often the method is used to indicate women's impatience with men's lack of commonsense (Fritz's in particular):

> 'That is my Söphgen to the life. It is Raphael's self-portrait, of course ... But how can a girl of twelve look like a genius of twenty-five?'
> 'That is easy,' said Sidonie. 'She cannot.' (*BF* 110)

Sidonie is right, of course, in a practical, rational way. But by making us laugh, her literal response to Fritz's love-drunk question allows us to look more kindly upon the lover and his feelings than we might otherwise have done. James Wood speaks of the task of the writer, reader and critic being to 'search for the irreducible, the superfluous, the margin of gratuity, the element in a style which cannot be easily reproduced and reduced'.[41] It is in Fitzgerald's rare combination of emotional insight and her metaphysical vision of a transcendent world cloaked in physical beauty that this irreducibility lies. In *The Blue Flower*, the greatest of her books, this combination results in a particular tonal quality that Fitzgerald found in J. L. Carr's *A Month in the Country*: 'a nostalgia for something we never had, "a tugging of the heart – knowing a precious moment gone and we not there"'[42] (*HA* 387). To read *The Blue Flower*, then, is partially at least to experience 'Sehnsucht', just as the book itself, indefinable and inexhaustible, rewarding multiple re-readings, concerns itself so profoundly with the embodiment of the concept in the lives of Novalis and those he knew. More, then, by far, as are all of Fitzgerald's late novels, than mere historical fiction.

5

Short Stories, Poems, Letters

Penelope Fitzgerald is primarily known as a novelist and biographer, and as a consequence her short stories are often overlooked. Fitzgerald herself played down her work in this form: 'I've never been able to write short stories. In my whole life I've only written three, and then only because I was asked to. It took me almost as long to finish one as to write a novel' (*HA* 472). Reviewers have been more enthusiastic, seeing Fitzgerald's short fiction as a distillation of her talent, constituted of 'that blend of truthful observation and deadpan comedy that stamped everything she wrote'.[1] Continuities with the novels certainly exist. Fitzgerald's tragicomic wit, art of compression, taste for the macabre and the 'illusion of total specificity' are all present in her short stories, as are the themes of misunderstanding, disappointment and loneliness. Yet reading the stories is a recognizably different experience to reading the novels. The sense of disruption of the accepted order of things is concentrated in the stories to the point of menace; the enigmatic presence of the author is sufficiently pervasive that the reader, though immersed in plot and character, can never quite forget that the stories have been *written*; and the moral, emotional or intellectual kernel of each story, often explicitly foregrounded, is invariably displaced, overshadowed or turned to irony by an unexpected and unfathomable turn. Fitzgerald's short stories, then, produce effects specific to the form, but the question asked so often of the novels applies here too: how does she do it? This chapter suggests that the secret lies in Fitzgerald's uncanny ability to know precisely how much or how little to reveal (tellingly, her preferred title for her collection of short stories was *Not Shown*). This ability underpins three particularly distinctive devices in Fitzgerald's short fiction: the way in which seemingly minor details come to assume major significance; brief interjections or interruptions in the flow of narration that alter the reader's perception of a story's realism; the strange process by which charismatic minor characters divert attention from the ostensible theme or motif of the story and leave the most lasting impression.

It is not known precisely how many stories Fitzgerald wrote. Some draft work probably sank in the Thames with *Grace*, the family's houseboat, and Fitzgerald herself didn't keep copies of her short stories (*SI* 515). Of those pieces that do survive, however, at least twenty-one separate published stories, loosely defined, can be identified – considerably more in any case than three. Early, uncollected short stories include as many as six written for *Cherwell* at Oxford in the 1930s, four published in various places in the 1950s, and one in the 1980s. In addition to these eleven, ten stories were collected in the paperback edition of *The Means of Escape* (2001), with dates of composition ranging from the 1970s to the late 1990s. The six Oxford pieces are recognizably Fitzgerald's – farcical, absurd stories told in a deliberately ironical manner but without the trademark pathos of her later work.[2] The four that date to the 1950s include a pair of spoof letters that appeared in the *World Review* in 1951, 'A Letter from Tisshara' and 'The Feast of the Writers in Tisshara', poking fun at the pretensions of the British Council, PEN, and writers' festivals.[3] 'The Mooi', thought to date to 1958, is an experimental monologue written in the style of Beckett's novels, published posthumously in 2008.[4] Dean Flower and Linda Henchey plausibly speculate that Fitzgerald might also have partly or even wholly written 'The Soldier in My Throat' in 1957, a comic sketch reminiscent both of *Punch* and *The Diary of a Nobody*, attributed to Desmond Fitzgerald when it was published in the monthly arts magazine, *Lilliput*.[5] A further uncollected story, 'Worlds Apart', published in *Woman* in 1983 when Fitzgerald was working on her biography of *Charlotte Mew*, is a story of love between two lonely people, Hester and Ernst. Hester's internal debate echoes that of Nenna James in *Offshore*, and the strategic, happiness-inducing deceit practised by Hester's daughter Tilly is reminiscent too of Tilda James's flexible attitude to truth (*PF* 291).[6] Three further stories listed by

Fitzgerald as possible inclusions in *The Means of Escape* – 'The Victoria Line' (1922, written when Fitzgerald would have been six years old), 'Matilda, Matilda' (1926, when she would have been ten), and 'The Find' (1955) – do not survive, and other short works were planned but never written.[7]

The earliest of Fitzgerald's stories are characterized by their cheerful experimentalism, sardonic confidence, cherishing of oddness, love of the chilling, and the literariness of their texture. They are closest in sensibility to the satirical playfulness of *The Golden Child*, though parallels can also be found in Fitzgerald's other early novels. Taken as a group, these stories show Fitzgerald principally in the guise of witty satirist, very much in the spirit of *Punch*, only revealing brief glimpses of the distinctive fusion of wit and feeling for which her novels are known. The ten stories collected in *The Means of Escape*, however, written over a forty-year span, contain elements both of the jocose sketch-writer and the offbeat irony and pathos of her later novels. The majority of the stories take place abroad and have some sort of period setting. Like her novels, a number of these tales draw on Fitzgerald's own experiences of work or travel: 'Beehernz' recalls a visit to Iona, 'The Red-Haired Girl' a summer holiday on the Cherbourg peninsula (*PF* 420). Others arise from her literary interests and writing projects: both 'The Prescription' and 'The Likeness' are linked to Fitzgerald's unwritten Istanbul novel, *The Iron Bridge*, and 'The Axe' clearly owes a debt to Herman Melville's 'Bartleby: The Scrivener'. All take their form from a recurring habit of thought in Fitzgerald's writing: 'I recalled closed situations that created their own story out of the twofold need to take refuge and to escape, and which provided their own limitations' (*HA* 498). Yet how, out of these closed situations and shared motivations, did Fitzgerald create stories that like her novels haunt the imagination and expand in the mind after first reading?

Subversion of expectations is a key to her method. In 'The Prescription' (1982), set in Istanbul, the reader expects the hard-working Greek apprentice to gain his revenge over the tyrannical Turkish master. Everything in the story points to this outcome. Instead, the apprentice is publically disgraced for deceit, prompting the reader to re-evaluate his or her own sense and standards of right and wrong. But reversals of expectation are not only confined to plotting. Another class of example, more glancing and less obviously intentional, is the way in which an apparently unremarkable piece of detail or colour comes to affect the reader more profoundly than the main events of the story. 'Our Lives Are Only Lent To Us', possibly written after Fitzgerald's journey to Mexico in 1952, appears to be a cautionary tale about the failure of communication between communities, Mexican and expatriate, and the mutual suspicion and, ultimately, hopelessness, this engenders. Yet Fitzgerald's skilful plotting discloses a more piercing, less certain grief. A caged starling voices what the reader later comes to realize are the anguished words of an unhappy, first wife: 'My God I can't bear it. My God I must get out.' Glimpses of the marriage are vouchsafed in short bursts – "Get out you bitch," trilled the starling' (*ME* 131) – and later we are told that the husband marries again. Whether the first wife is divorced or dead, however, we don't know. By comparison with these sinister hints, the story's ostensible motif – ' "*Venimos prestados*" she said, "Our lives are only lent to us" ' (*ME* 129) – seems depersonalized and moralizing, and even more so for being repeated sententiously at the story's end. Whether Fitzgerald meant it or not, it is the starling's harsh mimicry of the distraught first wife, rather than the story's reiterated maxim, that haunts the reader long after the story is over. There is nothing quite like this in Fitzgerald's novels, where specific details or moments tend to be more fully subsumed into the larger narrative.

The author's pervasive presence in Fitzgerald's short stories, and the manner in which it is insinuated, is also central to the experience of reading these works. In one sense this is hardly surprising: with so little time in a short story for the fictional world to seize the imagination, the reader invariably remains conscious of the authorial hand however deft it may be. Naturally enough, Fitzgerald does everything she can to diminish or distract from this awareness, not least through the inclusion of carefully disposed names, dates and curious facts or idioms, what V. S. Pritchett called 'the right details'. Thus 'The Means of Escape' begins:

> St George's Church, Hobart, stands high above Battery Point and the harbour. Inside, it looks strange and must always have done so, although (at the time I'm speaking of) it didn't have the blue, pink

and yellow-patterned stained glass that you see there now. That was ordered from a German firm in 1875. But St George's has always had the sarcophagus-shaped windows which the architect had thought Egyptian and therefore appropriate (St George is said to have been an Egyptian saint). They give you the curious impression as you cross the threshold, of entering a tomb. (*ME* 3)

The assembly of architectural features, recounted from an eye-witness perspective, bear out Pritchett's view that, 'Details make stories human, and the more human a story can be, the better'.[8] Having created such fully imagined settings for her stories, however, Fitzgerald's authorial voice then intrudes in some stories in ways that it never does in her novels. In 'Desideratus' (1997), set in late seventeenth-century England, a poor boy, Jack Digby, loses, then finds, a gilt medal he has been given. As time passes, Jack wonders how much money he might have made by selling the medal. The narrator comments:

> Anyone who has ever been poor – even if not as poor as Jack Digby – will sympathize with him in this matter. (*ME* 157)

The sentiment here is clearly borne of Fitzgerald's own experience, and prompts the reader to think both about the story and about the *form* of the story: who is telling me this tale, and why? The dividing line between author and narrator in this case is hard to discern. In 'At Hiruharama' (1992), by contrast, where the story is told in the third person in the voice of Mr Tanner, the interjection is made by the narrator, not the author. Early on Tanner says that his grandfather couldn't read or write, yet later he has his grandfather writing a letter to his sister'. – But wait a minute, surely he couldn't read or write? Evidently by that time he could' (*ME* 89). Who is speaking here? That it is the narrator, Mr Tanner, catching himself in a contradiction as storytellers do, becomes clear enough in the following lines. But a more important end has been achieved through this sudden interjection than simply the recording of Tanner's second thoughts. This brief moment of narrative doubt, seemingly hardly worth mentioning, has an effect that ripples through the rest of the story. The moment itself is so brief that the reader's absorption in the story is not shaken. Yet at the same time the moment is just disruptive enough to remind the reader of the presence of the author, producing the curiously satisfying effect, akin to a waking dream, of being aware of being immersed in the story *despite* it being a fiction. Most distinctive of all, Fitzgerald's short stories generate a sense of mystery and suggestion darker and more Gothic than the atmosphere of the novels, while avoiding the excesses of the 'creaky old machine of terror' found in *The Castle of Otranto, The House of Usher* and Jünger's *On the Marble Cliffs*: 'everything in these works exists between two worlds, one to be accounted for in the dialect of common sense... and the other world, subject to incursions of supernatural evil'.[9] Fitzgerald's 'ghost story', 'The Axe', provides an obvious example of this combination of the eerie and the everyday, as the reader comes gradually to appreciate the narrator's disturbed state of mind. In 'The Means of Escape', set in mid-nineteenth-century Tasmania, the menacing encounter between the Rector's daughter, Alice Godley, and the convict, Savage, breathes the same literary air of horror and death: 'the head was hidden in some kind of sack like a butchered animal, or, since it had eyeholes, more like a man about to be hung' (*ME* 5). 'Desideratus', however, meaning 'desired', named after an unfinished romance by William Morris, contains a scene that, because it is less amenable to interpretation than these, is even more strange and disquieting. Having lost his medal, Jack Digby realizes that it must have ended up at Watching, a lonely, great house at the bottom of the valley. At the house, Jack is told by a servant that 'God has not blessed Mr Jonas or either of his late wives with children'. Mr Jonas himself leads Jack to the cold 'dark upper floors', 'like a sepulchre, or a barn at the end of winter' (*ME* 155). In a bedroom, a boy with reddish hair lies in a linen gown, his back to Jack:

> 'You may go near him, and see him more clearly,' Mr Jonas said. 'His arm is hanging down, what do you make of that?'
> 'I think it hangs oddly, sir.' (*ME* 156)

Mr Jonas turns the inert boy's wrist until the fingers open. He returns the medal to Jack.

> 'Was it warm or cold?' they asked him later. Jack told them that it was cold. Cold as ice? Perhaps not quite as cold as that. (*ME* 156)

Hermione Lee thinks that the red-headed boy is 'sick' (*PF* 421), but the cold room and the motionlessness of this 'whiteish heap on the bed' may suggest even worse. But why then is there a tutor in the house? Might the boy have died just days or even hours before Jack arrived in search of his medal? And who is the boy if what the servant says is true, that 'God has not blessed Mr Jonas or either of his late wives with children'? Are we in the realm of a *doppelgänger*, as Terence Dooley sees it, wherein 'a resourceful boy wrest[s] the coin he has been given from the pallid ghost of his weaker self'? (*SI* xli). No answers are given, leaving each reader to draw his or her own conclusions.

This kind of interpretative inscrutability, arising here from the withholding of information, is produced in other stories by a quite different method: the stealthy, and often comprehensive, take-over of the story by one of Fitzgerald's cast of remarkable scene-stealers. In 'At Hiruharama', set on a remote farm in New Zealand, the story's centre of gravity shifts when the Tanners' neighbour Brinkman appears, come for his six-monthly dinner. He is one of Fitzgerald's lonely men who 'continued with the course of his thoughts, which were more real to him than the outside world's commotion' (*ME* 92). While Tanner's wife is giving birth in the bedroom, Brinkman, reminiscent of Selwyn Crane in *The Beginning of Spring*, waits patiently in the kitchen for his dinner, saying to the nurse: 'I think of myself as one of the perpetually welcome' (*ME* 94). As the story draws to its close and the narrator's point is made – that from such an unpromising beginning his aunt went on to do very well, becoming a lawyer in Wellington – it is Brinkman, not Tanner, who has the last thought, as the story swims back and forth from third-person narration to free indirect speech in its final sentences:

> Two more women born into the world! It must have seemed to him that if this sort of thing went on there should be a good chance, in the end, for him to acquire one for himself. Meanwhile, they would have to serve dinner sometime. (*ME* 95)

The effect of the aptly named Brinkman's late entrance into the story, and the impression left of his imperturbable, immovable presence, 'as solid as his chair' (*ME* 94), is both comic and oddly unruly, somehow casting into shade Mr Tanner's tale and its tinplate motto, 'Throw Nothing Away', by allowing a glimpse of a stranger, more potent, because less moral and logical, form of literary representation.

One final example, from 'The Means of Escape', demonstrates the effect on the reader of such a narrative takeover. Alice Godley, who is said to be doted upon by the Rector's housekeeper, Mrs Watson, makes careful preparations to escape with the convict Savage to England. But Savage fails to show up at the appointed hour. Eight months later a letter arrives from Portsmouth explaining how Savage had been diverted from Alice's window to Mrs Watson's:

> But I was made to pause at once by a Window opening and an Ivory Form leaning out, and a Woman's Voice suggesting a natural Proceeding between us, which there is no need to particularise. (*ME* 20)

This is an amusing, gratifyingly surprising twist, but the concealed shock comes in a different realization: that perhaps Mrs Watson had not after all welcomed Alice's attempts to teach her to write and read, and that 'her imitation, sometimes unconsciously grotesque, of Alice's rapid walk' (*ME* 14) might in fact have been intended as mockery. The reader is left feeling deeply uneasy and forced to question his or her understanding of the story up to that point. Mrs Watson never writes to explain why she took Alice's place in escaping from Tasmania with a convict, and so her motives, as Fitzgerald puts it dryly, '– which, taking into account her intense affection for Alice, must have been complex enough – were never set down and can only be guessed at' (*ME* 20–1). This could be the motto for all of Fitzgerald's short stories.

If Fitzgerald's short stories are in some ways even more enigmatic than her novels, then her poems, by contrast, few in number and most published posthumously, are surprisingly intimate and self-revealing, though not necessarily in the way one might guess. Her numerous reviews of poetry for *Punch* show a particular appreciation for Georgian lyricism, yet her own poems are a far cry from the poetic romanticism of Heinrich Heine or the mysterious music and wistful evocations of favourites Walter de la Mare and A. E. Housman. The earliest of Fitzgerald's poems, 'The Veteran', which appeared in her school magazine, the *Wycombe Abbey Gazette*, in 1936, when she was seventeen, is a mock-heroic portrayal of the life and tragic death of a milkman's horse, in the style of her father's light verse.[10] The next, a ten-line poem first published in *World Review* in 1950, is an elegy marking the death of George Bernard Shaw. Written in Fitzgerald's unsentimental manner, the poem ironically commends Shaw's success in living long enough to see his dark prophecies come true: 'And not the easy angel of failure with willow-green tears / But bitter success appeared in the long old age.'[11] It is possible that two further poems, both published unsigned in *World Review*, might also be by Fitzgerald. The first, a translation of Vincente Aleixandre's 'Como El Vilano' ('Like the Thistledown'), on the evanescence of young love, is included in an editorial article on 'The Arts in Modern Spain', signed by 'P. M. F. & D. F.'. The second, which precedes an editorial by Desmond Fitzgerald, is a threnody for George VI, depicting his funeral and the crowds that came. The poem is a concatenation of echoes, of T. S. Eliot 'Journey of the Magi', and of Genesis 3:19 ('for dust thou art, and unto dust shalt thou return'), and interpolates verbatim a couplet from 'Death the Leveller' (ll. 7–8) by seventeenth-century poet and playwright James Shirley.[12] The tone achieved here, and in all of these early poems, is that of the literate, feeling, sometimes humorous but always cerebral, observer and elegist.

Fitzgerald's poems written later, in the 1960s, thirteen of which were published in the *London Review of Books* in 2002, are noticeably different. Two of these poems, 'The Father and the Mother' and 'The Kitchen Drawer Poem', were later reproduced alongside 'Autumn: Departure of Daughters'.[13] A further short poem, 'Feeling and Reason', was published in 2013 (*PF* 213). Still markedly analytical, Fitzgerald's poems from this period, typed out with illustrations on each facing page, inspired by her daughter Tina's Paul Klee doodles, and bound into a book for family circulation, have been described as 'laconic…dry, quirky and bleak', in the manner of Fitzgerald's friend Stevie Smith (*PF* 212). But crucially, Fitzgerald personifies abstractions in these poems to convey deeply held responses to the people and world around her, which is rarely the case in her earlier, *Punch*-inspired verse. 'Feeling and Reason' is a good example of this latter kind:

> Feelings are treacherous
> Reason speaks truly.
> Good-morning, Reason,
> Good-morning, bully.

Another of Fitzgerald's personification poems, 'The Kitchen Drawer Poem', went on to be a finalist in the 1969 Poetry Festival in St John's, Smith Square, and Fitzgerald took pleasure in painting a comic picture of the reading: 'many of the contestants cheated and read very long poems about priests and sex and oppression and snow-queens'.[14] All of these poems are mordant, small-scale, occasional pieces, only partly successful. Sometimes oddly uneven in tone (such as 'Late Autumn: The Prophet at the Bus Stop'), and often echoing other poems and poets, such as Dorothy Parker's 'Self-Pity with Everything' ('Grease is undignified, / Vinegar's sordid'), Fitzgerald's poems still often succeed in defying expectation.

'The White Square Letter Poem'

1. From time to time no letters came
addressed correctly. He
saw there was one which never came
each morning punctually.

2. The curious sound a letter makes
not falling on the mat
not white not square he thinks he could
give some idea of that.

3. The white square look a letter has
not coming not again
is like a square white drop of blood
that runs back up the vein.

4. At 9 at 12 at 6 o'clock
on Saturdays at 3
his white square letter does not come
most conscientiously.

We can admire Fitzgerald's extension through four stanzas of the poem's clever conceit: the timing, sound and look of letters *not* arriving. But the poem is poignant as well as clever, owing to the deft pairing of painful subject matter with the kind of multisyllabic rhymes beloved of comic versifiers, from Samuel Butler to Cole Porter.

Poets and poetry feature too in Fitzgerald's prose works. Rossetti, Kipling, William Allingham and Swinburne, 'mad and deafening with excitement' (*EB* 67), Hilaire Belloc, G. K. Chesterton, Walter Headlam (*KB*) and Charlotte Mew all make appearances in the biographies, while Novalis and Selwyn Crane's *Birch Tree Thoughts* feature in the novels:

> 'Dost feel the cold, Sister Birch?'
> 'No, Brother Snow,
> I feel it not.' 'What? not?' 'No, not!'
>
> (*BS* 98)

As A. S. Byatt observed of this verse: 'Only a writer with a very good ear could have produced [such] exemplary dotty lameness'.[15] However, in Fitzgerald's own poems the comforting and familiar accoutrements of her novels and biographies – character, psychology and narrative – are stripped away, confronting the reader, disconcertingly at times, with a starker, more private version of Fitzgerald's authorial persona.

Fitzgerald's letters, collected in *So I Have Thought of You*, provide the student of her life and writing with a quite different, unmediated view of her personality. Of course, even letters written to family and friends, never intended for publication, are still rhetorical constructions and should be understood as such. Naturally enough, Fitzgerald accommodates herself to each correspondent in her letters, whether writing to her daughters, old or new friends, literary editors or fellow writers. Nonetheless, the authorial personality conveyed in Fitzgerald's letters is remarkably consistent in her interests, sympathies and sense of humour. The letters contain family news, literary gossip, discussions between author and publisher, and reveal information about Fitzgerald's habits of writing. A letter to literary editor Stuart Proffitt in 1993 explains the origin of 'At Hiruharama': 'I heard the story from a New Zealander when we were being rebaptized in the Jordan (or one of its sources, the one the Methodists favour anyway) marvellous wild cyclamen on the banks' (*SI* 431). This is typical of Fitzgerald's epistolary style: brimming with specific points of interest, an ecclesiological afterthought here, a delighted observation of nature there. In her letters to literary friends, ideas for books and writing projects provide surprising insights into her tastes and opinions. A letter to the American bibliographer Howard Woolmer reveals an unexpected liking for the Imagist poet F. S. Flint, and, though Fitzgerald had been fond of Stevie Smith, 'yet I truly think Anna Wickham was a more interesting poet' (*SI*

335–8). As other critics have noted, the humour in Fitzgerald's letters belongs firmly in the tradition of *Punch*, which she imbibed from her father, her uncle Ronald, and by writing for the magazine itself. The Grossmiths's *Diary of a Nobody*, which Fitzgerald read countless times, is also a clear influence on her depiction of the hapless, accident-prone 'Daddy' (Desmond Fitzgerald), as is E. M. Delafield's 'Robert' in *Diary of a Provincial Lady*, who is similarly 'laconic, impassive and discouraging'.[16]

The letters contain cheek by jowl almost every aspect of Fitzgerald's life – her literary and cultural interests, family worries and frictions: 'Maria has depressed me by 1. Looking at Daddy and me and saying: "What a funny old couple you are!" and 2. Telling me that studying art and literature is only a personal indulgence and doesn't really help humanity or lead to anything, and, I suppose, really, that is quite true: she said it very kindly. My life seemed to be crumbling into dust' (*SI* 58). Flashes of the Knox temperament are discernible beneath the restraint, 'Malcolm Bradbury said a few kind words to me about The G. of A., and I felt like throwing the pale green mayonnaise over him. I'm not sure that all these tests of character aren't too much, as one gets older' (*SI* 425). But such moments are greatly outnumbered by comic observations on popular culture: 'Quite exhausted by emotions raised by Eurovision Song Contest: We felt sure Cliff should have won, though doubtful about his dress of nylon ruffles and dandy's velvet-effect suit. It was very odd Germany suddenly giving 6 votes for Spain, I'm sure it was a vote to promote trade. (Wollen Sie in Spanien gehen?)' (*SI* 56). The wit, intelligence and acute observation of the critical writing, biographies and fiction is all here, but poured out in different measures according to the taste of each letter's recipient. The letters, then, give us Penelope Fitzgerald both 'at home' and 'at work', but for someone so addicted to writing and to depicting the world in all its astounding variety there was, really, little or no separation between them.

6

Reputation and Influence

Compared to Patrick O'Brian and Anthony Powell, famous English novelists who, like Fitzgerald, died in 2000, Penelope Fitzgerald's reputation is a relatively modest one. Neither her name nor her works, with the possible exception of *The Blue Flower*, are well known to the general public, yet what Fitzgerald's reputation lacks in reach it makes up for in intensity. To her admirers, many of whom are fellow writers, no praise is too high: 'There is a growing body of opinion that views Penelope Fitzgerald (1916–2000) as the pre-eminent English novelist of the late twentieth century, one whose novels in their artistry and grace bear comparison to those of Jane Austen and Virginia Woolf'; and, even more emphatically: 'Of all the novelists in English of the last quarter-century, she has the most unarguable claim on greatness.'[1] Evidence of the growth in Fitzgerald's posthumous reputation comes in various forms.

The appearance in 2013 of Hermione Lee's award-winning biography, *Penelope Fitzgerald: A Life*, published by Chatto & Windus, and the reissue of Fitzgerald's writing in 2013–14 by HarperCollins (Fourth Estate) constitute a significant commitment by these publishers to invest in Fitzgerald's work and reputation, reflecting their confidence in her continuing appeal. Fitzgerald's books have also been translated into numerous languages and adapted for other media. *The Blue Flower* and *Human Voices* have both been dramatized for radio and further adaptations are thought to be in the offing: among them a theatrical version of *At Freddie's* and a film of *The Bookshop*, a Spanish-British co-production directed by Isabel Coixet, to be released in 2017.[2] Fitzgerald and her novels also regularly feature in the 'best of' lists of literary journalists. In 2008 *The Times* included Fitzgerald as one of 'The 50 greatest British writers since 1945',[3] in 2012 *The Blue Flower* was named in *The Observer* as one of 'the ten best historical novels',[4] and in 2015 *The Beginning of Spring* was included in *The Observer*'s 100 best English-language novels of all time.[5] High-profile literary enthusiasts for Fitzgerald's work include Kate Atkinson, Julian Barnes, A. S. Byatt, Sebastian Faulks, Alan Hollinghurst and Philip Hensher.[6] Fitzgerald's high standing in such company prompts predictably sour responses. As a *Times* writer sarcastically observed: 'Certain things are a *sine qua non* of being a true intellectual, such as liking the novels of Penelope Fitzgerald.'[7] A useful corrective to this view comes from Richard Ollard, Fitzgerald's former editor, who warned against thinking that Fitzgerald's work is appreciated only by the *cognoscenti*: 'Penelope Fitzgerald delighted perhaps a wider range of readers than any novelist of her time. She was admired and enjoyed by every novel reader, but also by people who generally never read a novel at all.'[8] This claim, though difficult to prove, challenges the received wisdom that first and foremost Fitzgerald is 'a writer's writer' and not a popular one. Indeed, enshrined in standard literary and historical reference works such as the *Oxford Companion to English Literature* and the *Oxford Dictionary of National Biography*, Fitzgerald is manifestly not an obscure figure. Yet despite all of these accolades her place in the canon of twentieth-century and contemporary English fiction is far from secure. Two major academic surveys, *Contemporary British Women Writers* (2004) and *The Contemporary British Novel* (2004, 2007), fail even to mention Fitzgerald or her works.[9]

Academic studies of her writing are rare. Aside from Lee's biography, scholarly attention paid to Fitzgerald's writing to date comprises a monograph, a handful of journal articles and book chapters, and a doctoral thesis on her career and reputation.[10] In Fitzgerald's lifetime her novels were taught in England, Italy, China and the US, but this is less so now. Fitzgerald wryly commented: 'I used to go round and give little talks (quite uselessly, as the candidates always told me I couldn't be right because it wasn't what they'd got down in their notes).'[11] Literary fashions and tastes change, of course, but it is also true that Fitzgerald is an author whom educators and scholars find difficult to categorize among British writers of the late twentieth century. This is partly because her style and sensibility have more in common with her chronological peers, such as post-war novelists Barbara Pym, Muriel Spark and Iris Murdoch, than with novelists of the 1980s and 1990s.[12] At the same time, Fitzgerald's fiction refuses to fit into convenient literary critical moulds: 'People write to me: "In what sense are your books feminist?" As a matter of fact, they aren't feminist at all. "Are they post-modernist?" No. I point out that it would be better not to study them.'[13] Fitzgerald's polite but firm discouragement of budding scholars of her work reflects her frustration with the narrowly formulaic approach taken by some academic literary criticism. But the difficulty of categorizing Fitzgerald's work is also, in part, the difficulty of evaluating the work of a particular kind of contemporary female writer. The prize-winning career of the novelist Jane Gardam offers a useful point of comparison.

Both Fitzgerald and Gardam explore fundamental questions about the meaning, responsibilities and experience of life itself but proceed by subtle hints and 'the exquisite touch, which renders ordinary commonplace things and characters interesting', rather than seize readers by the lapels with the 'big bow-wow strain'.[14] The risk of such quiet virtues being disregarded is as great or greater when they are recognized and named (as 'elegance', 'miniaturism', or 'gentle irony') as when they are entirely misunderstood or overlooked. At the same time, reviewers of female ironists such as Fitzgerald or Gardam frequently overplay the benignity of their fiction, as though subtlety and understatement invariably connote a kind of fuzzy feminine mildness and calm. The evidence of Fitzgerald's novels, short stories, poems and letters, argues otherwise: 'Her work is actually much stranger and darker: it gives one just that sense of waste that is given by life itself.'[15]

What will be her legacy? Writers' reputations are notoriously difficult to predict, subject as they are to a thousand vagaries of culture, economics and taste. Reviewing a biography of Virginia Woolf, Fitzgerald cited Noel Annan's tongue-in-cheek assessment of Bloomsbury on the 'stock exchange of culture': 'Stracheys reached a high between the two wars, but suffered a catastrophic decline in the 1950s and 1960s and have never totally recovered their one-time value.... On the other hand, Forsters have proved to be remarkably firm right up to the 1980s, although they have eased somewhat since then' (*HA* 277). In the same vein, if the price of Penelope Fitzgeralds is currently on the rise then much is owed to Lee's biography for keeping her name before the public and to HarperCollins for keeping her work in print. Traces of Fitzgerald's influence can be found in novels by Julian Barnes, Philip Hensher and others, though she can be a hard act to follow: 'her style being similarly inclined to colloquialism and formality; her perspective at once worldly and estranged, benevolent but tart'.[16] The fusion of such apparently contradictory features of style and outlook produces, as this book has tried to show, the distinctive character of Fitzgerald's work, 'the element in a style which cannot be easily reproduced and reduced', which Fitzgerald would have called 'wit', and which is most distinctively manifested in her work in understatement, restraint and constant subversion of expectations. *How* Fitzgerald did it – how the novelist could have 'fifty pairs of eyes, plus "some secret sense as fine as air"' allowing her to move inside and outside her characters (*HA* 284) and enabling her readers in turn to lose themselves in each novel's fictional world, which, as Fitzgerald put it of reading a novel, 'is what I always hope for' (*HA* 422) – may be explained to some extent by close examination of the writing itself and the process of composition. As this book has tried to show, the evidence of Fitzgerald's working papers suggests that if a 'not-herself' took possession of the writer, then it was only as a result of infinite pains and study.

Explanation, though, is not the same as understanding. Partly because Fitzgerald's writing is so elusive, her style so difficult to emulate, it is unlikely that there will ever be a school of Penelope Fitzgerald as there was once thought to be one of Beryl Bainbridge. And without new work appearing with its attendant publicity there is a risk that Fitzgerald's idiosyncratic voice, as cherished as it is by her devoted followers, may fade and disappear, like those of contemporaries such as A. L. Barker, or novelists of an earlier generation such as May Sinclair. At the foot of Fitzgerald's grave in the graveyard of Hampstead Parish Church, St John's, where her ashes are interred next to those of her father and stepmother, is inscribed the first line of

Henry Vaughan's visionary poem, 'They are all gone into the world of light', a line marked in Fitzgerald's copy of Vaughan's poems (*PF* 430–1). If Fitzgerald is to become, as Thomas Hardy said of Charlotte Mew, a writer 'who will be read when others are forgotten' (*CM* 181), then schools and universities must take up her work, playwrights and screenwriters must continue to adapt her writing, and publishers of literary classics, such as Penguin, Faber or Oxford University Press, should include her books in their lists. Our literary culture is, and will be, an immeasurably richer, more surprising and sharply tender place for it.

Appendix: Uncollected and Unattributed Poems

'G. B. S.'

Childless old fellow, you fell from the apple tree
And your million children drew their breath in pain.

You are the only one left, for ever spared to them
While the gas flickered out and the street was lit with atoms.

Ninety-four years not being too long a reminder
That there is a human mind in the human body.

And not the easy angel of failure with willow-green tears
But bitter success appeared in the long old age.

To make all you thought of come true, said the bitter angel,
And still he will not give in, say his million children.

P. M. F.[1]

'Como El Vilano', by Vincente Aleixandre

Lovely is the Kingdom of love
But bitter also is the Kingdom.
It is because the lover's heart
Is bitter in the lonely hours apart
Watching the inaccessible cloud of air
He sees her eyes are there

The lover is born for happiness
For propagation everlasting
Which from his innermost heart unfolds
To lose itself for ever and ever
In the pure heart of love delivered

But the solicitous round of life
The nagging hours day by day
And that same airy cloud, and dreams
And the short flight of the young whom love inspires
All whisper against the duration of the impossible fires.[2]

'The Queue'

It was a story for childen's children
A winter's tale of the death of a King –
When the heard-of died, the unheard stood in their thousands
In the sootblack frostwhite night before spring.

Lights on the bridge, the dazzled dark
River ran between fire and fire
With sensible shoes and ruined faces
They crawled towards their heart's desire.

They were blind in the icy breath,
To the nightlong thought of majesty
Goldringed goldrobed envied apart
But as thou art so he shall be
    And in the dust be equal made
    With the poor crooked scythe and spade

But the day and the night, and the day and the night
War borne, war torn, care shared, dead in the prime,
Their own dust shaken, their dear heart breaking,
They cared for this, in winter time.[3]

Notes

INTRODUCTION

1. P. M. Fitzgerald, 'On Reading E. M. Forster', *Punch*, 207/5418 (22 Nov 1944), 448–9.
2. 'Place aux Dames: In the News, Miss Penelope Knox (Somerville)', *Isis*, 19 (May 1938), 10.
3. P. M. Knox, 'Olympia: The International Horse Show', *Punch*, 196/5125 (28 Jun 1939), 714. 'P. M. Knox' will be given as PMK in all subsequent references; 'P. M. Fitzgerald' will be given as PMF.
4. The adage appears to derive from E. R. Calthrop's *The Horse, as Comrade and Friend* (London: Hutchinson, 1921), 39: 'All horses are fit for heaven, but only a few men'. A decade later, the saying was sufficiently well established to be quoted by the 12-year-old Sarah Bowes-Lyon in her *Horsemanship as it is Today* (London: Dent, 1933), Preface.
5. PMF, *WR*, n.s. 18 (Aug 1950), 5.
6. Interview with Fitzgerald in Nicholas A. Basbanes, *Patience and Fortitude: Wherein a Colorful Cast of Determined Book Collectors, Dealers, and Librarians Go About the Quixotic Task of Preserving a Legacy* (New York: HarperCollins, 2001), 239.
7. George Steiner, *Language & Silence: Essays on Language, Literature and the Inhuman* (New York: Atheneum, 1967), ix.
8. James Wood, 'Late Bloom', review of Hermione Lee, *Penelope Fitzgerald: A Life, New Yorker* (24 Nov 2014), 128.
9. Stoppard, 'Pragmatic Theatre', *NYTBR* (23 Sep 1999), quoted by Wendy Lesser, 'Penelope', in Zachary Leader (ed.), *On Modern British Fiction* (Oxford: Oxford University Press, 2002), 108; the religious poet Evelyn Underhill's description of listening to a Charlotte Mew recital (*CM* 111).
10. PMF, 'The Man in the Back Row has a Question V', *Paris Review*, 40/146 (Mar 1998), 163. Meiosis is another word for litotes (ironical understatement).

11. See *OED*, 'wit', *n.* II.8a.
12. Caroline Moorhead, 'A Modest Mistress of Words', interview of PMF, *The Times*, 62559 (10 Sep 1986), 19.
13. Eleanor Wachtel, interview with PF, *Writers & Company*, Canadian Broadcasting Company (21 Apr 1996). See also Julian Gitzen, 'Elements of Compression in the Novels of Penelope Fitzgerald', *Essays in Arts and Sciences*, 26 (1 Oct 1997), 13. The evidence of Fitzgerald's working papers suggests that her remark about cutting first drafts in half applies only to her later novels, from *Innocence* onwards.
14. HRC, box 2, folder 1.
15. Dean Flower, 'A Completely Determined Human Being', *HR*, 57/4 (2005), 583.
16. PMF, *WR*, n.s. 50 (Apr–May 1953), 17, 18, 22, 28.
17. A. S. Byatt, 'A Delicate Form of Genius', *Threepenny Review* (Spring 1998); PMF, 'The Feminine Genius', *Punch*, 213/5580 (3 Dec 1947), 542.
18. PMK, 'Words and Pictures', *Punch*, 203/5305 (21 Oct 1942), 346.

CHAPTER 1. CRITICAL WRITING

1. Edmund Gordon, 'C'est qu'elle a vécu: The unknown Penelope Fitzgerald', *TLS*, 5596 (2 Jul 2010), 14–15.
2. Dean Flower, 'A Completely Determined Human Being', *HR*, 57/4 (2005), 581–92. In 1939 Fitzgerald contributed two pieces to the *TLS* (see Dean Flower and Linda Henchey, 'Penelope Fitzgerald's Unknown Fiction', *HR*, 61/1 (Spring 2008), 53).
3. PMF, *WR*, n.s. 38 (Apr 1952), 72.
4. PMK, 'At the Play', *Punch*, 203/5291 (22 Jul 1942), 60.
5. PMF, 'The Feminine Genius', *Punch*, 213/5580 (3 Dec 1947), 542; 'Wie Schwarz Sind Deiner Blätter', *Punch*, 204/5330 (14 Apr 1943), 319; 'Phantoms and Atoms', *Punch*, 210/5479 (2 Jan 1946), 318.
6. PMF, *WR*, n.s. (28 Jun 1951), 60, 63.
7. PMF, 'On Reading E. M. Forster', *Punch*, 207/5418 (22 Nov 1944), 448–9).
8. PMF, 'Word-gathering', *Punch*, 206/5375 (9 Feb 1944), 124.
9. PMF, 'Variations on an English Theme', *Punch*, 206/5382 (29 Mar 1944), 276.
10. PMF, 'Stonier on the War', *Punch*, 205/5362 (10 Nov 1943), 404.
11. PMF, 'Individualists', *Punch*, 207/5412 (18 Oct 1944), 340.
12. PMK, 'At the Pictures', *Punch*, 199/5185 (7 Aug 1940), 142–3.
13. PMF, 'At the Play' (review of Robert Sherwood's 'There Shall Be No

Night'), *Punch*, 206/5370 (5 Jan 1944), 16.
14. PMF, *LRB* (1988); *HA* 245.
15. PMF, 'Walk Up', *Punch*, 204/5319 (27 Jan 1943), 82.
16. PMK, 'At the Pictures', *Punch*, 199/5194 (9 Oct 1940), 356.
17. PMK, 'At the Pictures', *Punch*, 199/5185 (7 Aug 1940), 142–3.
18. PMF, 'The Literature of Pursuit', *Punch*, 205/5349 (18 Aug 1943), 146–7.
19. PMK, 'At the Pictures', *Punch*, 199/5199 (6 Nov 1940), 448.
20. PMF, review of Barbara Jones, *The Unsophisticated Arts*, *WR*, n.s. 36 (Feb 1952), 70.
21. Introduction to J. L. Carr, *A Month in the Country* (*HA* 386).
22. PMF, 'The Feminine Genius', *Punch*, 213/5580 (3 Dec 1947), 542.
23. PMF, '"Ex Africa..."', *Punch*, 205/5351 (1 Sep 1943), 190–1.
24. PMK, 'At the Pictures', *Punch*, 199/5196 (23 Oct 1940), 400–1.
25. PMF, *WR*, n.s. 42 (Aug 1952), 19, 14.
26. PMF, *WR*, n.s. 50 (Apr–May 1953), 17.
27. PMF, 'A Battered Caravanserai', *Punch*, 207/5399 (19 Jul 1944), 60–1.
28. PMF, 'Variations on an English Theme', *Punch*, 206/5382 (29 Mar 1944), 276.
29. Penelope Knox, 'War on Wit', *TLS*, 1933 (18 Feb 1939), 105. The characters cited here are: Millamant, from Congreve's *The Way of the World* (1700); Lord Henry, from Oscar Wilde's *Dorian Gray*; Zuleika Dobson, from Max Beerbohm's novel of the same name; Mrs Mountstuart Jenkinson, from George Meredith's *The Egoist*.
30. PMF, 'Fantasy in Earnest', *Punch*, 205/5364 (24 Nov 1943), 449.
31. PMF, '"Turn that Darned Thing Off..."', *Punch*, 206/5389 (17 May 1944), 426.
32. PMF, 'Two Poets', *Punch*, 207/5421 (13 Dec 1944), 512–13.
33. PMF, 'The Listener', *Punch*, 209/5473 (28 Nov 1945), 470.
34. PMF, 'Roses in the Waste Land', *Punch*, 204/5317 (13 Jan 1943), 40.
35. PMF, 'Spring Poetry', *Punch*, 208/5433 (7 Mar 1945), 212.
36. PMF, *WR*, n.s. 32 (Oct 1951), 76.
37. PMF, 'Roses in the Waste Land', *Punch*, 204/5317 (13 Jan 1943), 40.
38. PMF, 'New Writing and Twilight', *Punch*, 212/5538 (12 Feb 1947), 178.
39. PMF, '"If Snow Would But Stay Put..."', *Punch*, 214/5610 (23 Jun 1948), 546.
40. PMF, '"Even in Spring..."', *Punch*, 209/5457 (15 Aug 1945), 146–7.
41. PMF, 'Poems of Pity', *Punch*, 210/5487 (6 Mar 1946), 212. Fitzgerald does, however, point out that in discussing Robert Herrick, Sitwell 'disregards almost entirely the changes in English vowel-sounds over the last five centuries' ('A Poet's Miscellany', *Punch*, 204/5337 (21 Jun 1943), 470).

42. PMF, *WR*, n.s. 35 (Jan 1952), 79, 12.
43. PMF, *WR*, n.s. 42 (Aug 1952), 19, 14.
44. PMF, 'More Britain in Pictures', *Punch*, 204/5326 (Mar 17 1943), 232–33.
45. PMF, 'Spring Poetry', *Punch*, 208/5433 (Mar 7 1945), 212.
46. HK, 'Thomas Hardy', *Punch*, 202/5274 (1 Apr 1942), 272.
47. Other notable contributors included: William Saroyan, L. P. Hartley, Michael Hamburger, Joyce Cary, Dannie Abse, John Lehmann, Iain Hamilton, Harold Macmillan, Herbert Read, W. S. Graham, Patrick Galvin, Julien Gracq, Robert Gittings, Robert Conquest, Donald Davie, Alan Brownjohn, Francis King, Anthony Thwaite and names now less well known, such as Milo Cripps and Inez Holden.

CHAPTER 2. BIOGRAPHIES

1. Other writers' lives reviewed or introduced by Fitzgerald include those of Edward Benson, Lewis Carroll, Edward Lear, Christina Rossetti, Walter de la Mare, George Moore, Radclyffe Hall, Dorothy Sayers, Dora Carrington, Ford Madox Ford, Alain-Fournier, Rebecca West, Jean Rhys, Evelyn Waugh, Louis MacNeice, C. S. Lewis, Angus Wilson and Roald Dahl.
2. PMF, 'The Great Romantic', *Punch*, 209/5462 (19 Sep 1945), 255.
3. Letter to Francis King, 28 Jan [1978] (*SI* 264).
4. Letters to Mary Lago, New Year's Day 1987, 9 Jul [1994] (*SI* 313, 319).
5. Letter to Harvey Pitcher, 18 Apr [1988] (*SI* 443–4).
6. See John Ruskin, 'The Queen of the Air' (1869), in *Selected Writings*, ed. Dinah Birch (Oxford: Oxford University Press, 2004), 179, 180.
7. In her recent biography of Burne-Jones, Fiona MacCarthy comments that fresh archival research has made it 'possible to arrive at a much fuller account of Burne-Jones's family relationships and sexual history, especially his devastating love affair with Maria Zambaco' (*The Last Pre-Raphaelite: Edward Burne-Jones and the Victorian Imagination* (London: Faber & Faber, 2011), xxiii).
8. Fitzgerald always made it clear that *KB* was a biography of the *brothers*, which is why she makes little mention of her two aunts, Ethel and Winifred. See *PF* 20–3.
9. The technical parts of Fitzgerald's account of Dilly's cryptographic work on Enigma were drawn from Gustave Bertrand, author of *Enigma* (1973). For trenchant criticism of the report's technical accuracy, see Mavis Batey, *Dilly: The Man Who Broke Enigmas*

(London: Biteback Publishing, 2010), 163.
10. Ethel Knox, 'Mothering famous people', *Daily Chronicle* (12 May 1930); Evelyn Waugh, *Ronald Knox* (Bungay: Chapman & Hall, 1959), 4–6; and Batey, *Dilly*, 3–4.
11. *SI* 353. For example, Fitzgerald mentions but passes quickly over the exclusion of Ronnie from his father's will on account of Ronnie's conversion to Rome (*KB* 132, 256); see E. A. Knox, *Reminiscences of an Octogenarian, 1847–1934* (London: Hutchinson, 1934), 300, and David Rooney, *The Wine of Certitude: A Literary Biography of Ronald Knox* (San Francisco: Ignatius Press, 2009), 23. Evelyn Waugh's *Ronald Knox* makes no mention of the exclusion at all.
12. Postcard, 28 Jan [1978] (*SI* 263).
13. Letter to Richard Ollard, 8 May 1978 (*SI* 244).
14. PMF, *WR*, n.s. 38 (Apr 1952), 4.
15. Fitzgerald wrote about Mew on numerous occasions. See 'Charlotte Mew', *Oxford Dictionary of National Biography* (2004); review of Val Warner (ed.), *Charlotte Mew: Collected Poems and Prose*, in *LRB* (1982) (*HA* 171–84); and 'Introduction', Howard J. Woolmer, *The Poetry Bookshop: A Bibliography* (1988) (*HA* 154–70).
16. Alida Monro, 'Charlotte Mew – A Memoir', in *Collected Poems of Charlotte Mew* (London: Gerald Duckworth & Co, 1953), xii.
17. See Alida Monro, 'Charlotte Mew – A Memoir', viii; and Joy Grant, *Harold Monro and The Poetry Bookshop* (London: Routledge & Kegan Paul, 1967), esp. 64–5.

CHAPTER 3. EARLY NOVELS

1. A further autobiographical novel for which some notes survive ('Why (or 'How') We Were Very Young'), based on Fitzgerald's years at Oxford, was never written (*PF* 54–5).
2. See Peter Wolfe, *Understanding Penelope Fitzgerald*, 295–301; A. N. Wilson, 'Penelope Fitzgerald: The core of her mystery', *TLS* (5 Feb 2014).
3. Nicholas A. Basbanes, *Patience and Fortitude* (New York: Harper-Collins, 2001), 239.
4. Garamantians, whose civilization dates back from the fifth century BC, are found in Herodotus.
5. *Independent Books* (24 Sep 1994).
6. I am grateful to Arnold Hunt for this suggestion.
7. Lévi-Strauss's *Structural Anthropology* was first published in 1958, and translated into English in 1963; Derrida's *Of Grammatology* came

out in 1968; and Barthes's *S/Z* in 1970.
 8. PMF, '"Dark with Excessive Bright"', *Punch*, 213/5567 (10 Sep 1947), 260.
 9. PMF, 'The Romantic Allegory', *Punch*, 205/5345 (21 Jul 1943), 60–1.
10. See the last four lines of Stevens's poem: 'If her horny feet protrude, they come / To show how cold she is, and dumb. / Let the lamp affix its beam. / The only emperor is the emperor of ice-cream.'
11. Dean Flower and Linda Henchey, 'Penelope Fitzgerald's Unknown Fiction', *HR*, 61/1 (Spring 2008), 54. See Chapter 5 in this vol.
12. *Independent Books* (24 Sep 1994).
13. PMF, 'A Study of Roaring Farce', *WR*, n.s. 34 (Dec 1951), 10.
14. At the time of writing, such a restored edition is thought to be imminent; see Courtney Cook, 'Penelope Fitzgerald Was Here: An Appreciation', *LATBR* (23 Jan 2015).
15. PF interview, Diana Hinds, *Books and Bookmen*, 364 (Sep 1986), 34. Presumably in the interview Fitzgerald forgot, or chose not to mention, her ideas for *The Iron Bridge* or *Sale or Return*.
16. 'Curriculum Vitae' (*HA* 476).
17. Letter to PF, 10 Dec 1978 (HRC, box 4, folder 9). Mrs Neame took over the bookshop from Christopher Rowan-Robinson in 1958. Did Fitzgerald know that Phyllis Neame was the daughter of the popular novelist Guy Boothby, who wrote a series of books featuring Dr Nikola, an occultist criminal mastermind? No doubt Fitzgerald would have enjoyed the connection had she known.
18. Letter to PF, 10 Dec 1978 (HRC, box 4, folder 9).
19. Valentine Cunningham, 'Suffocating Suffolk', review of *The Bookshop*, *TLS*, 3998 (17 Nov 1978), 1333. When, almost two decades later, *The Bookshop* was published by Mariner Books in the US, Cunningham reviewed it again and praised it more fulsomely: 'a classic whose force as a piece of physical and moral map making has not merely lasted but has actually improved with the passage of years' ('Among the Proles and the Posh', review of *The Bookshop, NYTBR* (7 Sep 1997), 11–12). For a summary of the early reviews, see *PF* 266.
20. Gordon, 'The unknown Penelope Fitzgerald', *TLS*, 5596 (2 Jul 2010), 14.
21. James Wood, 'Late Bloom', review of Hermione Lee, *Penelope Fitzgerald: A Life, The New Yorker* (24 Nov 2014), 128–32.
22. 'Curriculum Vitae' (*HA* 478).
23. See Elizabeth Barrett Browning's *The Seraphim*, and Fitzgerald's echo of the epilogue's appeal to the poem's supernatural addressees: 'And lay upon their burning lips a thought / Damp

with the weeping which mine earth inherits.'
24. Gumbrecht, *Atmosphere, Mood, Stimmung: On a Hidden Potential of Literature*, trans. Erik Butler (Stanford, CA: Stanford University Press, 2012), esp. 1–22.
25. Frank Kermode, 'Booker Books', *LRB* (22 Nov 1979), 12–13.
26. Letter to Frank Kermode, 2 Nov 1979 (*SI* 452).
27. Fitzgerald herself began working at the BBC in December 1940, three years after graduating from Oxford. Hermione Lee suggests that most characters are recognizable figures: 'Mac' is like Ed Murrow or John McBain; Eddie Waterlow could be Eddie Sackville-West; The Halibut closely resembles Alvar Liddell; Dr Vogel is very like Ludwig Koch (*PF* 72).
28. Such communities included the British Museum in *The Golden Child*, the theatre school in *At Freddie's*, Fred Fairly's Cambridge college in *The Gate of Angels*, the print works in *The Beginning of Spring*, and the community of barge dwellers in *Offshore*.
29. Letter to Richard Ollard, 29 Feb 1980 (*SI* 278).
30. Fitzgerald's portrait of the dryly detached Haggard draws heavily upon her memories of her father, Evoe Knox, who had died just a few years before she began the novel.
31. Heine is quoted by Heinrich in *Offshore* (*OF* 119).
32. Fitzgerald explains in 'Curriculum Vitae' how closely Annie's experience of falling in love with no hope of return matched her own, when she worked at the BBC in the war (*HA* 475).
33. See George Ewart Evans, *Ask the Fellows Who Cut the Hay* (London: Faber & Faber, 1956; 2nd edn, 1975), 119.
34. A. S. Byatt, 'The Isle Full of Noises', *TLS*, 4043 (26 Sep 1980), 1057. See also Frank Kermode, 'The Duckworth School of Writers', *LRB*, 2/22 (20 Nov 1980), 19.
35. Fitzgerald gave an account of the stage school in 'Curriculum Vitae' (*HA* 479–80). See also Paul Bailey's hostile review in *The London Evening Standard* (1982).
36. Letter to Richard Ollard, 13 Apr 1982 (*SI* 391).
37. Simon Callow, 'Introduction', *At Freddie's* (London: Fourth Estate, 2013), xi.
38. John Sutherland, 'Nationalities', *LRB*, 4/8 (6 May 1982), 19; Anne Duchene, 'All for Loss', *TLS*, 4122 (1982), 32; Roxana Robinson, 'In Short: Fiction', *NYTBR* (8 Sep 1985), 24.
39. PMK, 'At the Revue', *Punch*, 203/5294 (12 Aug 1942), 126.
40. PF interview with Joan Acocella, *New Yorker* (7 Feb 2000), 86.

CHAPTER 4. LATE NOVELS

1. PMF, 'Art critic without a clue', *Independent* (23 Sep 1994).
2. As mentioned in Chapter 4, the designations 'early' and 'late' apply only to Fitzgerald's career as a novelist, though of course the four 'late' novels were all written at a late stage in Fitzgerald's life, in her eighth decade.
3. Wendy Lesser, 'Penelope', in Zachary Leader (ed.), *On Modern British Fiction* (Oxford: Oxford University Press, 2002), 111.
4. Michael Dibdin, 'Daring to dance through a minefield', *Independent on Sunday* (1 Oct 1995).
5. Christopher Ricks, *Eliot and Prejudice* (Berkeley and Los Angeles: University of California Press, 1988), 259.
6. Caroline Moorhead, 'A Modest Mistress of Words', *Times*, 62559 (10 Sep 1986), 19.
7. Francis King, review of *Innocence*, *Spectator* (12 Sept 1986), 33; Nicci Gerrard, review of *Innocence*, *Women's Review* (1986); C. K. Stead, 'Chiara Ridolfi', *LRB* (9 Oct 1988), 21–2.
8. Erich Auerbach, *Mimesis: The Representation of Reality in Western Literature*, trans. Willard R. Trask (Princeton: Princeton University Press, 1953; 2003), 535.
9. Letter to Richard Ollard, 2 Nov 1979 (*SI* 374).
10. HRC, box 2, folder 3.
11. HRC, box 7, folder 21.
12. Letter to Harvey Pitcher, 6 Mar 1988 (*SI* 442).
13. In an interview, Fitzgerald commented that 'for *The Beginning of Spring*, *The Gate of Angels*, and *The Blue Flower* I had a strong image in my mind which didn't necessarily appear, in one same form, in the novels, but persisted, all the same, right through the story'. (Lian Lu, 'Penelope Fitzgerald's Fiction and Literary Career: Form and Context' (unpublished PhD thesis, University of Glasgow, 1999), 293.)
14. MF, 'Pity Unlimited', *Punch*, 204/5331 (21 Apr 1943), 340–1.
15. Letter to Frank Kermode, 2 Nov 1979 (*SI* 452).
16. *Saturday Review*, 326/1 (16 Mar 1889).
17. HRC, box 6, folder 13.
18. Letter to Harvey Pitcher, 6 Mar 1988 (*SI* 442).
19. *A Vagabond in the Caucasus* (1911), *Undiscovered Russia* (1912), *A Tramp's Sketches* (1913).
20. See *Smiths of Moscow*, 36 and *The Beginning of Spring*, 7, 17.
21. *Smiths of Moscow*, 40–41, 87.
22. Fitzgerald told Frank Kermode in 1995 that she thought that Macdonald was the only person who had really understood

Novalis (*PF* 226).
23. PMF, *WR*, n.s. 22 (Dec 1950), 4.
24. HRC, box 4, folder 2.
25. A story Fitzgerald remembered from *Edward Burne-Jones*, 230.
26. 'PF vista por PF', in *British Writers at Alcalá de Henoses* Vol. I, ed. Ricardo Sola Buil and Luis Alberto LÃzaro, British Council (1995), 83–96 (qtd in *PF* 366).
27. HRC, box 3, folder 11.
28. Frank Kermode, *Penelope Fitzgerald: The Bookshop, The Gate of Angels, The Blue Flower* (London: Everyman, 2001), xvi.
29. Anita Brookner, 'Daisy pulls it off', *Spectator* (26 Sep 1990), 32.
30. 'All Praise to Thee, My God, This Night', music by Tallis, words by Ken. The lines in Kingsley's *Water Babies* read: 'God grant you find one face there, / You loved when all was young.'
31. D. H. Lawrence, *Three Novellas: The Ladybird, The Fox, The Captain's Doll* (Harmondsworth: Penguin, 1982), 156.
32. HRC, box 1, folder 7. For a fuller account of the origins of *BF*, see *PF*, 388–406.
33. Marilynne Robinson, referring to dreams, in *Housekeeping* (New York: Picador, 1980), 116.
34. Frank Kermode, 'Dark Fates', *LRB*, 17/19 (5 Oct 1995), 7.
35. Laura E. Savu, 'Writing in the Margins of an Endless Novel', *Postmortem Postmodernists: The Afterlife of the Author in Recent Narrative* (Cranbury, NJ: Fairleigh Dickinson University Press, 2009), 90.
36. I am indebted to Terence Dooley for this reference.
37. HRC, box 1, folder 7.
38. HRC, box 2, folder 4.
39. HRC, box 1, folder 10.
40. HRC, box 2, folder 7.
41. James Wood, *How Fiction Works* (London: Vintage, 2009), 175–6.
42. See Houseman's *A Shropshire Lad* (no. XXXII). 'I am here on earth only for a short time, Housman says. You must trust me. "Take my hand quick and tell me, / What you have in your heart."' (*HA* 383)

CHAPTER 5. SHORT STORIES, POEMS, LETTERS

1. Penelope Fitzgerald, *The Means of Escape* (London: Flamingo, 2001), iii (*The Age*, Australia).
2. The *Cherwell* stories include: 'A Curious Incident'; 'A Desirable Resident' (1937); 'The Curse of a Literary Education'; 'I Was Afraid'; 'Look Stranger'; 'Wicked Words'. See Dean Flower and Linda

NOTES

Henchey, 'Penelope Fitzgerald's Unknown Fiction', *HR*, 61/1 (Spring 2008), 47–65; Edmund Gordon, 'C'est qu'elle a vécu: The unknown Penelope Fitzgerald', *TLS* (2 Jul 2010); *PF* 59–60.

3. I follow Dean Flower and Linda Henchey in seeing Fitzgerald as the sole author of these pieces, despite the fact that the editorial is signed 'D. M. F. and P. M. F'. See Flower and Henchey, 'Penelope Fitzgerald's Unknown Fiction', 53–5.
4. 'The Mooi' was first published in *HR*, 61/1 (Spring 2008), 71–7; see Flower and Henchey, 'Penelope Fitzgerald's Unknown Fiction', 47–65; *PF* 121.
5. 'The Soldier in My Throat', *Lilliput*, 41/5 (Nov 1957), reprinted in *HR*, 61/1 (Spring 2008), 66–70. See Flower and Henchey, 'Penelope Fitzgerald's Unknown Fiction', 47–65. Flower and Henchey also speculate that Fitzgerald might have had a hand in her husband's book *A History of the Irish Guards* (1949).
6. 'Worlds Apart', *Woman* (1983); reprinted in *HR* 61/1 (Spring 2008), 78–86.
7. Flower and Henchey, 'Penelope Fitzgerald's Unknown Fiction'; *PF* 97, 303–4, 434.
8. Lorrie Moore, 'Ordinary Life Always Went Too Far', review of V. S. Pritchett, *A Careless Widow and Other Stories*, *New York Times* (22 Oct 1989), sect. 7, 3.
9. PMF, review of Julien Gracq, *The Castle of Argo*, *WR*, n.s. 35 (Jan 1952): 79; Frank Kermode, 'Playing the Seraphine', *LRB*, 23/2 (25 Jan 2001), 15.
10. Edmund Gordon, 'C'est qu'elle a vécu: The unknown Penelope Fitzgerald', *TLS* (2 Jul 2010).
11. PMF, 'G. B. S.', *WR*, n.s. 20 (Oct 1950), 7; *PF* 112. See Appendix.
12. 'Como El Vilano', *WR*, n.s. 22 (Dec 1950), 18; 'The Queue', *WR*, n.s. 37 (Mar 1952), 4. See Appendix. Neither poem can be attributed to Fitzgerald for sure, though no other candidate seems likely.
13. See 'The Father and the Mother', 'The Kitchen Drawer Poem', 'Jug Poem', 'The Two Lovers Poem', 'The White Square Letter Poem', 'A Lover's Humble Request', 'Arrival of a Stray Cat in the Poet's Lodgings', 'The Record Player Poem', 'Letter from a Creditor to a Poet', 'The Later Middle Ages', 'An Invitation from the Poet to Visit His Lodgings at 87a Underdone Road', 'Late Autumn; The Prophet at the Bus Stop' in 'Thirteen Poems by PF', *LRB* 26/19 (3 Oct 2002), 26–7; and 'Autumn: Departure of Daughters' (*SI* xvii, 522–4).
14. Letter to Tina, early 1969 (*SI* 62–3).
15. A. S. Byatt, 'A Delicate Form of Genius', *Threepenny Review* (Spring 1998).

16. Rosemary Hill, 'Making Do and Mending', *LRB*, 30/18 (25 Sep 2008), 9.

CHAPTER 6. REPUTATION AND INFLUENCE

1. Christopher J. Knight, '"Between the Hither and the Farther Shore": Penelope Fitzgerald's *Offshore*', *Logos: A Journal of Catholic Thought and Culture*, 17/1 (Winter 2014), 90; Philip Hensher, 'Perfection in a Small Space', review of *The Means of Escape*, *Spectator* (20 Oct 2000), 51.
2. Courtney Cook, 'Penelope Fitzgerald Was Here: An Appreciation', *LATRB* (23 Jan 2015).
3. *Times* (5 Jan 2008).
4. William Skidelsky, 'The 10 best historical novels', *Observer* (13 May 2012).
5. Robert McCrum, 'From Bunyan's Pilgrim to Carey's Kelly', *Observer* ('The New Review') (16 Aug 2015), 18–20.
6. Other well-known authors commissioned to write introductions for the Fourth Estate reissue include novelists such as Michèle Roberts, Candia McWilliam and Andrew Miller, the biographer Richard Holmes, actor Simon Callow, museum director Charles Saumarez Smith, and former controller of BBC Radio 4, Mark Damazer. Numerous other writers are champions of her work, including Harriet Harvey Wood, David Nicholls, Adam Mars-Jones, Salley Vickers, Rachel Joyce, John Lanchester, A. N. Wilson and Neel Mukherjee.
7. Catherine Nixey, *Times* (20 Dec 2014), Saturday Review; Features, 12.
8. Richard Ollard, Obituary of Penelope Fitzgerald, *Independent* (9 May 2000), 6.
9. Emma Parker (ed.), *Contemporary British Women Writers* (Cambridge: D. S. Brewer, 2004); Philip Tew (ed.), *The Contemporary British Novel* (London: Continuum, 2004; 2nd edn, 2007). I owe this observation to Stephanie Harzewski, 'New Voice, Old Body: the Case of Penelope Fitzgerald', *Contemporary Women's Writing*, 1/1–2 (2007), 24–33.
10. Peter Wolfe, *Understanding Penelope Fitzgerald* (Columbia, SC: University of South Carolina, 2004); authors of a number of recent scholarly articles on Fitzgerald's work include Dean Flower and Christopher Knight; Lian Lu, 'Penelope Fitzgerald's Fiction and Literary Career: Form and Context' (unpublished PhD thesis, University of Glasgow, 1999). A monograph by Christopher Knight

focussing on Fitzgerald's novels, *Penelope Fitzgerald and the Consolation of Fiction* (London: Routledge, 2016), was published as this present book was going to print. See Select Bibliography for other important articles and book chapters on Fitzgerald's life and writing.
11. Letter to Harvey Pitcher, 22 Jun 1995 (*SI* 450).
12. See Lian Lu, 'Penelope Fitzgerald's Fiction and Literary Career', 262–3. When *Offshore* won the Booker Prize in 1979, Fitzgerald was dismissed as 'a kind of lesser Barbara Pym' (see Hermione Lee, 'From the margins', *Guardian* (3 Apr 2010)).
13. Interview with Penelope Fitzgerald: Jonathan Sale, 'Passed/Failed: Penelope Fitzgerald', *Independent* (18 Feb 1999), Education, 7.
14. From Sir Walter Scott's review of Jane Austen's *Emma* (*The Journal of Sir Walter Scott*, Mar 1826).
15. Ian Sansom, 'Oh, Subtle', *Salmagundi*, 128/129 (Fall 2000/Winter 2001), 57.
16. Leo Robson, on Philip Hensher's literary debt to Penelope Fitzgerald, *Guardian* (12 Jul 2014).

APPENDIX: UNCOLLECTED AND UNATTRIBUTED POEMS

1. *WR*, n.s. 20 (Oct 1950), 7.
2. *WR*, n.s. 22 (Dec 1950), 18.
3. *WR*, n.s. 37 (Mar 1952), 4.

Select Bibliography

WORKS BY PENELOPE FITZGERALD

Biographies, novels, short stories, letters and critical writing

Edward Burne-Jones: A Biography (London: Michael Joseph, 1975; London: Hamish Hamilton, 1989; Stroud: Sutton, 2003; London: Fourth Estate, 2014)

The Knox Brothers (London: Macmillan, 1977; London: Harvill, 1991; London: Flamingo, 2002; London: Fourth Estate, 2013)

The Golden Child (London: Duckworth, 1977; Boston: Mariner Books, 1999; London: Harper Perennial, 2004; London: Fourth Estate, 2014)

The Bookshop (London: Duckworth, 1978; London: Flamingo, 1989; Boston: Mariner Books, 1997; London: Fourth Estate, 2013)

Offshore (London: Collins, 1979; London: Flamingo, 1988, 2003; Boston: Mariner Books, 1998; London: Fourth Estate, 2013)

Human Voices (London: Collins, 1980; London: Flamingo, 1988, 1997; Boston: Mariner Books, 1999; London: Fourth Estate, 2014)

At Freddie's (London: Collins, 1982; New York: Godine, 1985; London: Flamingo, 1989, 2003; Boston: Mariner Books, 1999; London: Fourth Estate, 2013)

Charlotte Mew and Her Friends: with a Selection of Her Poems (London: Collins, 1984; Reading, MA: Addison-Wesley, 1988; London: Harvill, 1992; London: Flamingo, 2002; London: Fourth Estate, 2014)

Innocence (London: Collins, 1986; Boston: Mariner Books, 1998; London: Flamingo, 2004; London: Fourth Estate, 2013)

The Beginning of Spring (London: Collins, 1988; London: Flamingo, 1989; Boston: Mariner Books, 1998; London: Fourth Estate, 2014)

The Gate of Angels (London: Collins, 1990; Boston: Mariner Books, 1998; London: Flamingo, 2004; London: Fourth Estate, 2014)

SELECT BIBLIOGRAPHY

The Blue Flower (London: Flamingo, 1995; Boston: Mariner Books, 1997; London: Fourth Estate, 2013)
The Means of Escape: Stories (London: Flamingo, 2000; Boston: Houghton Mifflin, 2000; Boston: Mariner Books, 2001)
The Bookshop; The Gate of Angels; The Blue Flower (intro.), Frank Kermode (London: Everyman's Library, 2001)
Offshore; Human Voices; The Beginning of Spring (intro.), John Bayley (London: Everyman, 2003)
The Afterlife: Essays and Criticism (New York: Counterpoint, 2003)
A House of Air (intro.), Hermione Lee (London: Harper Perennial, 2003). A collection of Fitzgerald's critical writing; for uncollected items, see below
So I Have Thought of You: The Letters of Penelope Fitzgerald ed. Terence Dooley (London: Fourth Estate, 2008)

Uncollected critical writing

See the endnotes for Penelope Fitzgerald's juvenilia, the many book, film and theatre reviews that she wrote for *Punch* 1937–1948, the reviews, editorial articles and features she wrote for *World Review*, 1950–1953, and the dozens of book reviews she wrote in the 1980s and 1990s, many of which are not included in *A House of Air* or *The Afterlife*.

Interviews

Basbanes, Nicholas A., 'The Traditionalist and the Revolutionary', interviews with Penelope Fitzgerald and Robert Coover, *Biblio: Exploring the World of Books*, 3/9 (Sept 1998), 10.
Charters, Mallay, 'Penelope Fitzgerald: A Voice Amidst the Blitz', *Publishers Weekly*, 246/20 (17 May 1999), 51–2. Interview conducted to coincide with US publication of *Human Voices*.
Durden-Smith, Jo, 'A Writer's Life', *Departures* (30 Mar 2010).
Gorb, Ruth, 'The Gentle Ghost of Keats in a Neighbour's Bathroom', *Express & News* (16 Nov 1979), 16.
Hinds, Diana, *Books and Bookmen*, 364 (Sept 1986).
Lennon, Peter, 'Men are Such Hopeless Creatures', *Guardian* (13 Apr 1998).
Lubow, Arthur, 'An Author of a Certain Age', *New York Times Magazine* (15 Aug 1999): sec. 6, 30–3.
Moorhead, Caroline, 'A Modest Mistress of Words', *Times*, 62559 (10 Sept 1986), 19. Contains Fitzgerald's brief but interesting account of the genesis of *Innocence*.
Reynolds, Annie, 'A book is a lovely thing', *Island*, 52 (Spring 1992), 38–41.

Roberts, Glenys, 'The Original Boat Person', *Evening News* (25 Oct 1979), HRC, box 1, folder 24.
Sale, Jonathan, 'Passed/Failed: Penelope Fitzgerald', *Independent* (18 Feb 1999), Education, 7. Brief profile piece in which Fitzgerald denies that her books are 'feminist' or 'post-modern'.
Wachtel, Eleanor, interview with Penelope Fitzgerald, *Writers & Company*, Canadian Broadcasting Company (21 Apr 1996).

Working papers

Penelope Fitzgerald Papers. Harry Ransom Humanities Research Center. University of Texas at Austin.

CRITICAL STUDIES

Books

Knight, Christopher J., *Penelope Fitzgerald and the Consolation of Fiction* (London: Routledge, 2016). Monograph focussing on Fitzgerald's nine novels.
Lee, Hermione, *Penelope Fitzgerald: A Life* (London: Chatto & Windus, 2013). Superbly detailed, sympathetic biography, shedding fresh light on Fitzgerald's intellectual contexts, motivations, working and family conditions. An indispensable aid for study.
Wolfe, Peter, *Understanding Penelope Fitzgerald* (Columbia, SC: University of South Carolina, 2004). First monograph on Fitzgerald's life and career. Contains intriguing conjectures about Fitzgerald's literary sources and allusions, though the author is not always attuned to Fitzgerald's sensibility; mistakes stoicism for failure and implausibly places the Balzac-inspired *The Bookshop* in the company of novels by Angry Young Men such as Kingsley Amis and John Braine.

Unpublished Thesis

Lu, Lian, 'Penelope Fitzgerald's Fiction and Literary Career: Form and Context' (PhD thesis, University of Glasgow, 1999), revised as, *Beyond The Text: Direction of Literary Study from Studying the Fiction and Literary Career of Penelope Fitzgerald* (University of Fudan, 2005). Interesting if slightly outdated exploration of Fitzgerald's writing career and literary reputation.

Articles and Chapters in Books

Acocella, Joan, 'Assassination on a Small Scale', *New Yorker* (7 Feb 2000), 80–8. Important profile article, containing useful discussion of the relationship between Fitzgerald's earlier and later fiction.

Adams, Don, 'There's a Providence Not so Far Away from Us: Penelope Fitzgerald's Parablistic Realism', in D. Adams, *Alternative Paradigms of Literary Realism* (New York: Palgrave, 2009), 123–86. Thought-provoking reading of Fitzgerald as 'a parablist': an author who shows through her fiction how one could and should live morally in the world.

Barnes, Julian, 'The Deceptiveness of Penelope Fitzgerald', in *Through the Window: Seventeen Essays (and One Short Story)* (London: Vintage, 2012), 1–14. Perceptive assessment of Fitzgerald's skill as a novelist.

Basbanes, Nicholas A., 'Profiles in Bibliophagia', in *Patience and Fortitude: Wherein a Colorful Cast of Determined Book Collectors, Dealers, and Librarians Go About the Quixotic Task of Preserving a Legacy* (New York: HarperCollins, 2001), 219–61.

Bawer, Bruce, 'A still small voice: the novels of Penelope Fitzgerald', *New Criterion*, 10/7 (Mar 1992), 33–42. Concise summary of Fitzgerald's novels up to *The Gate of Angels*, emphasizing their combination of realism and the transcendent.

Brookner, Anita, 'Thoughts on a dry brain in a dry season', *Spectator* (21 Jun 1996), 35. Insightful discussion of the fusion of research and imagination in Fitzgerald's novels.

Byatt, A. S., 'A Delicate Form of Genius', *Threepenny Review* (Spring 1998), 13–15. Perceptive analysis of Fitzgerald's insistence in her fiction on the individuality of each of her characters.

Clayton, Douglas, 'Penelope Fitzgerald 1916–2000', in *Modern British Women Writers: An A-to-Z Guide*, eds. Vicki K. Janik and Del Ivan Janik (Westport, CN: Greenwood Press, 2002), 123–8. Introductory overview of Fitzgerald's novels; useful emphasis on Fitzgerald's productive combination of realism and idealism.

Cook, Courtney, 'Penelope Fitzgerald Was Here: An Appreciation', *LATBR* (23 Jan 2015). Focused on the transformative effect on readers, especially women, of Fitzgerald's life and fiction. Personal, heartfelt.

Fleming, Bruce, 'Skirting the Precipice: Truth and Audience in Literature', *Antioch Review*, 56/3 (1998), 334–57. Sharply critical account of *The Blue Flower*, accusing Fitzgerald of asking her readers to accept too much on trust.

Flower, Dean, 'Ghosts, shadow patterns and the fiction of Penelope Fitzgerald', *HR*, 54/1 (2001), 133–40. Thoughtful essay that touches on the sources of Fitzgerald's moral vision and wit.

———, and Linda Henchey, 'Penelope Fitzgerald's Unknown Fiction', *HR*, 61/1 (Spring 2008), 47–65. Fascinating article discussing Fitzgerald's early fiction, some of which is printed in an appendix.

Gitzen, Julian, 'Elements of Compression in the Novels of Penelope Fitzgerald', *Essays in Arts and Sciences*, 26 (1 Oct 1997), 1–14. Illuminating essay on the strengths and weaknesses of Fitzgerald's style of characterization.

Gordon, Edmund, 'C'est qu'elle a vécu: The unknown Penelope Fitzgerald', *TLS*, 5596 (2 Jul 2010), 14–15. Informative article on Fitzgerald's early writing career, at school, university and in the first years of her marriage.

Harvey Wood, Harriet, Obituary of Penelope Fitzgerald, *Guardian* (3 May 2000), 22.

Harzewski, Stephanie, 'New Voice, Old Body: the Case of Penelope Fitzgerald', *Contemporary Women's Writing*, 1/1–2 (2007), 24–33. Critical analysis of common motifs in seventeen obituaries of Fitzgerald: sanctity, femininity, elegance, reserve, formal economy and personal modesty and thrift.

Hensher, Philip, 'A Long Leap to Perfection', review of *Penelope Fitzgerald: A Life* by Hermione Lee, *Guardian* (2 Nov 2013).

Hollinghurst, Alan, 'The Victory of Penelope Fitzgerald', review of Hermione Lee, *Penelope Fitzgerald: A Life*, *NYRB*, 61/19 (4 Dec 2014), 8–12.

Knight, Christopher J., 'XVI. Penelope Fitzgerald (*The Blue Flower*)', in *Omissions are Not Accidents: Modern Apophaticism from Henry James to Jacques Derrida* (Toronto: University of Toronto Press, 2010), 162–75. Wide-ranging essay on what is not said in *The Blue Flower*, and on the quality and effects of the mystery thereby evoked.

———, 'Penelope Fitzgerald's Beginnings: *The Golden Child* and Fitzgerald's Anxious Relation to Detective Fiction', *Cambridge Quarterly*, 41/3 (Sept 2012), 345–64. Examination of Fitzgerald's ambivalence regarding her contribution to detective fiction. Argues that detective fiction presents us with mysteries akin to those of a spiritual nature, challenging and not readily resolved; in this sense, all of Fitzgerald's fiction can be viewed as a form of detective fiction.

———, 'The Second Saddest Story: Despair, Belief, and Moral Perseverance in Penelope Fitzgerald's *The Bookshop*', *Journal of Narrative Theory*, 42/1 (Winter 2012), 69–90. Interesting essay that pinpoints mourning as the unstated theme of *The Bookshop*. Suggests that the novels that follow continue to work through Fitzgerald's experience of mourning her husband.

———, 'Concerning the Unpredictable: Penelope Fitzgerald's *The Gate of Angels* and the Challenges to Modern Religious Belief', *Religion & Literature*, 45/3 (Autumn 2013), 25–57.

———, '"Between the Hither and the Farther Shore": Penelope Fitzgerald's *Offshore*', *Logos: A Journal of Catholic Thought and Culture*, 17/1 (Winter 2014), 90–111. Discusses the origin of *Offshore* and the themes of 'betwixtness' and numinosity. The latter theme is examined in relation to the matter of prayer and of evidencing divinity.

———, 'Penelope Fitzgerald's *At Freddie's*, or "All My Pretty Ones"', *Critique: Studies in Contemporary Fiction*, 57/2 (2016), 123–36. Interesting essay arguing that in *At Freddie's* Fitzgerald expresses her deep concern about adult neglect or mistreatment of children.

Knox, E. A., *Reminiscences of an Octogenarian, 1847–1934* (London: Hutchinson, 1934).

Lee, Hermione, 'From the margins', *The Guardian* (3 Apr 2010). Fascinating piece on Fitzgerald's working library.

Lesser, Wendy, 'Penelope' in Zachary Leader (ed.), *On Modern British Fiction* (Oxford: Oxford University Press, 2002), 107–25. Identifies three key features of Fitzgerald's novels: her ability to write from within a particular culture; wit that seems to emanate from the characters themselves; a highly productive relationship between the short duration of the events of the novel and the far longer passage of time within which those events are placed.

Lewis, Tess, 'Between Head and Heart: Penelope Fitzgerald's Novels', *New Criterion*, 18/7 (2000), 29–36. Overview of the novels, focussing on the 'moral force' of Fitzgerald's imagination.

McCrum, Robert, '*Penelope Fitzgerald: A Life* by Hermione Lee – review', *Observer* (17 Nov 2013).

MacLeod, Lewis, '"You Might Not Call Penelope Fitzgerald a Feminist Writer, but She Is One": On Gender and the Discourse of Certitude in *Offshore*', *Critique: Studies in Contemporary Fiction*, 57/2 (2016), 107–22. Comparative analysis of the fiction of Fitzgerald and J. M. Coetzee, exploring why no particular type of critical approach seems appropriate when considering Fitzgerald's work. Offers a subtle feminist reading of *Offshore*, responsive to the book's ironic critique of masculine claims to certitude.

Ollard, Richard, 'Fitzgerald [*née* Knox], Penelope Mary (1916–2000)', *Oxford Dictionary of National Biography*, Oxford University Press, 2004; online edn, Sep 2012 [http://www.oxforddnb.com/view/article/74141, accessed 28 Mar 2016].

———, Obituary of Penelope Fitzgerald, *Independent* (9 May 2000), 6.

Rooney, David, *The Wine of Certitude: A Literary Biography of Ronald Knox* (San Francisco: Ignatius Press, 2009).

Sansom, Ian, 'Oh, Subtle', *Salmagundi*, 128/129 (Fall 2000/Winter 2001), 48–57. Valuable corrective to the tendency to eulogize Fitzgerald for the subtlety and detail of her writing; Sansom argues that her fiction is stranger and darker than usually recognized.

Savu, Laura E., 'Writing in the Margins of an Endless Novel', *Postmortem Postmodernists: The Afterlife of the Author in Recent Narrative* (Cranbury, NJ: Fairleigh Dickinson University Press, 2009), 74–105. Savu finds in *The Blue Flower* a 'postmodern suspicion of linear temporality, closure, unity, and absolutes'; she argues that these features in *The Blue Flower* reinforce Novalis's view of life as an 'endless novel'.

Smith, Dinitia, 'Penelope Fitzgerald, Novelist, Is Dead at 83', *New York Times* (3 May 2000), B10.

Stonebridge, Lyndsey, 'Hearing Them Speak: Voices in Muriel Spark, Wilfred Bion and Penelope Fitzgerald', *Textual Practice*, 19/4 (Dec 2005), 445–65. Reads *Human Voices* not only as defence of the dissemination of truth in politically compromised times, but also as a powerful political critique in its own right of the elitist and anti-democratic senior management of the BBC in the 1940s.

Stoppard, Tom, 'Pragmatic Theatre', *NYTBR* (23 Sept 1999).

Sudrann, Jean, 'Magic or Miracles: The Fallen World of Penelope Fitzgerald's Novels', in Robert E. Hosmer Jr (ed.), *Contemporary British Women Writers: Texts and Strategies* (Basingstoke: Macmillan, 1993), 105–27. Oft-cited overview of Fitzgerald's first seven novels.

Taylor, D. J., 'Booker: musical chairs with quirky comers', *Independent* (20 Oct 1990), 10.

Turner, Jenny, 'In the Potato Patch: Review of *Penelope Fitzgerald: A Life* by Hermione Lee', *LRB* (19 Dec 2013), 3–8.

Turner, Nick, *Post-War British Women Novelists and the Canon* (London: Continuum, 2010). Focuses on Iris Murdoch, Anita Brookner, Ruth Rendell and Emma Tennant, only briefly discussing Fitzgerald; insightful, nonetheless, about inherent difficulties in predicting the future reputation of any given writer.

Waugh, Evelyn, *The Life of the Right Reverend Ronald Knox* (Bungay: Chapman & Hall, 1959).

Wilson, A. N., 'Penelope Fitzgerald: The core of her mystery', review of Hermione Lee, *Penelope Fitzgerald: A Life*, *TLS* (5 Feb 2014), 3–4.

Wood, James, 'Late Bloom', review of Hermione Lee, *Penelope Fitzgerald: A Life*, *New Yorker* (24 Nov 2014), 128–32.

Selected reviews of Fitzgerald's books

Annan, Gabriele, 'Death and the Maiden', review of *The Blue Flower*, *TLS*, 4824 (15 Sept 1995), 20.

SELECT BIBLIOGRAPHY

Astor, Judy, 'Children in Trouble', review of *At Freddie's*, *Listener*, 107/2755 (8 Apr 1982), 23–4.
Bailey, Paul, review of *At Freddie's*, *London Evening Standard* (1982).
Bayley, John, 'Innocents at Home', review of *The Gate of Angels*, *NYTRB* (9 Apr 1992), 13–14.
Binyon, T. J., 'Goldrush', review of *The Golden Child*, *TLS*, 3941 (7 Oct 1977), 1134.
Brookner, Anita, 'Moscow before the Revolution', review of *The Beginning of Spring*, *Spectator* (1 Oct 1988), 29–30.
——, 'Daisy pulls it off', review of *The Gate of Angels*, *Spectator* (26 Sept 1990), 31–2.
Byatt, A. S., 'The Isle Full of Noises', review of *Human Voices*, *TLS*, 4043 (26 Sept 1980), 1057.
Callendar, Newgate, 'Crime', review of *The Golden Child*, *NYTBR* (1 Apr 1979), 21.
Chamberlain, Lesley, 'Worried, Norbury', review of *The Beginning of Spring*, *TLS*, 4460 (23 Sept 1988), 1041.
Clapp, Susannah, 'Finishing Touches', review of *Charlotte Mew and her Friends*, *LRB* (20 Dec 1984), 20.
——, 'Suburbanity', review of *The Golden Child*, *New Statesman* (10 Oct 1977), 483.
Corn, Alfred, 'Broadcast News', review of *Human Voices*, *NYTBR* (9 May 1999), 7.
Cunningham, Valentine, 'Among the Proles and the Posh', review of *The Bookshop*, *NYTBR* (7 Sept 1997), 11–12.
——, 'Suffocating Suffolk', review of *The Bookshop*, *TLS* (17 Nov 1978): 1333.
Davis, Barbara Beckerman, '*The Means of Escape: Stories*', *Antioch Review* 60/1 (Winter 2002), 163–4.
Diski, Jenny, 'Elements of an English Upbringing', review of *The Knox Brothers*, *American Scholar* (Autumn 2000), 140–2.
Duchene, Anne, 'Do No Evil, Mean No Evil', review of *Innocence*, *TLS*, 4354 (12 Sept 1986), 995.
Duguid, Lindsay, 'In Faery Lands Forlorn', review of *Edward Burne-Jones*, *TLS*, 4988 (6 Nov 1998), 10.
Eder, Richard, 'Innocence', *LATBR* (3 May 1987), 3–4.
——, 'Two Bicycles, One Spirit', review of *The Gate of Angels*, *LATBR* (12 Jan 1992), 3, 7.
——, 'Penelope Fitzgerald, Her Family's Eyes and Heart', review of *The Knox Brothers*, *New York Times* (31 Aug 2000).
Flower, Dean, 'A Completely Determined Human Being', *Hudson Review*, 57/4 (2005), 581–92. Review article of *The Afterlife: Essays and Criticism* (2003), containing interesting discussion of Fitzgerald's

career as a literary critic.
Gardam, Jane, 'The Professor and the Flower', review of *The Blue Flower*, *Spectator* (23 Sept 1995), 38.
Glendinning, Victoria, 'Between Land and Water', review of *Offshore*, *TLS* (23 Nov 1979), 10.
Gross, John, 'Books of the Times', review of *Innocence*, *NYTBR* (28 Apr 1987), 17.
Haughton, Hugh, 'Witness to the Real Thing', review of *Charlotte Mew and Her Friends*, *TLS*, 4255 (19 Oct 1984), 1190.
Hay, Elizabeth, 'Penelope Weaves Her Last Fictional Web', *Globe and Mail* (Toronto) (2 Dec 2000), D9.
Heller, Zoe, 'Affairs of the Heart in Defiance of Reason', review of *The Gate of Angels*, *Independent* (25 Aug 1990), 29.
Hensher, Philip, 'Perfection in a Small Space', review of *The Means of Escape*, *Spectator* (20 Oct 2000), 51.
——, 'The Sweet Smell of Success', review of *The Blue Flower*, *Spectator* (11 Apr 1998), 33–4.
Herzog, Dagmar, 'Love in the Time of Tuberculosis', review of *The Blue Flower*, *Women's Review of Books* (Oct 1997), 6–7.
Hill, Rosemary, 'Making do and mending', review of *So I Have Thought of You*, *LRB* (2008), 9–10.
Himmelfarb, Gertrude, 'A God-Haunted Family', review of *The Knox Brothers*, *New Republic* (16 Oct 2000), 59–65.
Hofmann, Michael, 'Nonsense Is Only Another Language', review of *The Blue Flower*, *NYTBR* (13 Apr 1997), 9.
Holmes, Richard, review of *The Blue Flower*, 'Paradise in a Dream', *NYRB* (17 Jul 1997), 4.
Hosmer, Robert E. Jr., 'Appraising *At Freddie's*', *NYTBR* (6 Oct 1985), 42.
Jones, Louis B., 'When People Collide', review of *The Gate of Angels*, *NYTBR* (20 Dec 1992), 7.
Kellaway, Kate, 'Atoms, Angels and the Mach Factor', review of *The Gate of Angels*, *Observer* (12 Aug 1990), 50.
——, 'A Bicycle Made for Two', review of *The Gate of Angels*, *Listener* (23 Aug 1990), 24.
Kermode, Frank, 'Booker Books', review of *Offshore*, *LRB* (22 Nov 1979), 12–13.
——, 'The Duckworth School of Writers', review of *Human Voices*, *LRB* (20 Nov–4 Dec 1980), 18.
——, 'Dark Fates', review of *The Blue Flower*, *LRB* (5 Oct 1995), 7.
——, 'Playing the Seraphine', review of *The Means of Escape*, *LRB* (25 Jan 2001), 15.
King, Francis, review of *Innocence*, *Spectator* (12 Sept 1986), 33
King, Nina, 'The Heart Has Its Reasons', review of *The Gate of Angels*,

Washington Post: Book World (23 Feb 1992), 1.
Lee, Hermione, 'Down by the Thames', review of *Offshore*, *Observer* (2 Sept 1979), 37.
——, 'Listening Carefully', review of *The Means of Escape*, *TLS*, 5090 (20 Oct 2000), 22.
Leider, Emily, 'In Short: Fiction', review of *Innocence*, *NYTBR* (10 May 1987), 20.
Longford, Frank, 'A Unique Quartet of Brothers', review of *The Knox Brothers*, *Contemporary Review* (Apr 1978), 216–18.
Mannes-Abbott, Guy, 'Angelic Voices', review of *The Blue Flower*, *New Statesman* (6 Oct 1995), 38.
Muggeridge, Malcolm, 'A Family and its Humour', review of *The Knox Brothers*, *TLS*, 3944 (28 Oct 1977), 1256.
Newby, P. H., 'BBC Seraglio', review of *Human Voices*, *Listener* (2 Oct 1980), 445.
Noe, Mark D., 'Fitzgerald's *The Beginning of Spring*', *Explicator*, 59 (2001), 204–6.
O'Donoghue, Bernard, 'A Passionate Humanity', review of *A House of Air*, *TLS*, 5258 (9 Jan 2004), 5.
Owens, Jill T., 'Charlotte Mew', review of *Charlotte Mew and Her Friends*, *English Literature in Transition 1889–1920*, 32/2 (1989), 229–32.
Parini, Jay, 'Companionship was Everything', review of *Charlotte Mew and Her Friends*, *NYTBR* (7 Aug 1988), 15.
Penner, Jonathan, 'Moscow on the Eve', *Washington Post: Book World* (1 Jun 1989), 1.
Plunket, Robert, 'Dear, Slovenly Mother Moscow', review of *The Beginning of Spring*, *NYTBR* (7 May 1989), 15.
Pritchard, William H., 'Tradition and Some Individual Talents', *HR*, 45/3 (Fall 1992), 481–90.
Raban, Jonathan, 'The Fact Artist', review of *Human Voices*, *New Republic* (2 Aug 1999), 39–42.
Reynolds, Gillian, 'Auntie at War', review of *Human Voices*, *Punch* (15 Oct 1980): 28.
Reynolds, Susan Salter, 'Human Voices', *LATBR* (6 Jun 1999), 11.
Robinson, Roxana, 'In Short: Fiction', review of *At Freddie's*, *NYTBR* (8 Sept 1985), 24.
Rumens, Carol, 'Assaults on the Rational', review of *The Gate of Angels*, *New Statesman* (1 Sept 1990), 31–2.
Scurr, Ruth, 'Shelf life', review of *So I Have Thought of You*, *TLS*, 5499 & 5500 (22 & 29 Aug 2008), 3–5.
Stead, C. K., 'Chiara Ridolfi', review of *Innocence*, *LRB* (9 Oct 1988), 21–2.
Stuewe, Paul, 'Innocence', *Quill and Quire*, 53/2 (Feb 1989), 27.

Thwaite, Anthony, 'Stagers Old and New', review of *At Freddie's*, *Observer* (28 Mar 1982), 31.
Wagner-Martin, Linda, 'Madness and Gentility', review of *Charlotte Mew and Her Friends*, *American Book Review*, 10/6 (1989), 21.
Walker, J. K. L., 'Bringing Spirit and Matter Together', review of *The Gate of Angels*, *TLS*, 4560 (24 Aug 1990), 889.
Walters, Margaret, 'Women's Fiction', review of *The Beginning of Spring*, *LRB* (13 Oct 1988), 20-2.
Ward, Elizabeth, 'Love in Florence', review of *Innocence*, *Washington Post: Book World* (12 Jul 1987), 4.
Wheeler, Edward T., 'A Listener's Guide', review of *Human Voices*, *Commonweal* (10 Sep 1999), 32–4.
———, 'Ronnie & the boys', review of *The Knox Brothers*, *Commonweal* (3 Nov 2000), 32–4.
Williamson, Barbara F., 'Quiet Lives Afloat', review of *Offshore*, *NYTBR* (13 Sept 1987), 51.

Index

Works are indexed under the names of their authors.

Abse, Dannie 123 n. 47
Acocella, Joan 126 n. 40, 135
Addison, Joseph 16
Alain-Fournier [Henri-Alban Fournier] 6, 123 n. 1
Aleixandre, Vincente: 'Como El Vilano' 109, 118–19, 129 n. 12
Allingham, William 110
Annan, Noel 115
Arts and Crafts movement 22
Ashbee, C. R. 21
Atkinson, Kate 114
Auden, W. H. 18
Austen, Jane 4, 13, 47, 60, 79, 113

Bainbridge, Beryl 5–6, 93, 116
Baldwin of Bewdley, Lord 25
Balzac, Honoré de 134: *Le Curé de Tours* 44, 47
Barker, A. L. 6, 116
Barker, George 18
Barnes, Julian 77, 114, 116, 135
Barrett Browning, Elizabeth: *The Seraphim* 125 n. 23
Barrie, J. M. 82
Barthes, Roland 39, 125 n. 7
Bassani, Giorgio 19, 69
Baum, Vicki 10, 14
Baylis, Lilian 61
Beaton, Cecil 14

Beckett, Samuel 4, 77, 102
Belloc, Hilaire 110
Benson, Edward 123 n. 1
Bernhardt, Sarah 23
Betjeman, Sir John 19
Bible 2, 27, 51
Blakemore, Michael 61
Blunden, Edmund 19
Boothby, Guy 125 n. 17
Boothroyd, Basil 19
Bootsie and Snudge 52
Botticelli, Sandro: *Primavera* 69
Bowen, Elizabeth 10, 13
Bradbury, Malcolm 112
Briggs, Asa 48
British Broadcasting Corporation (BBC) 3, 5, 20, 38, 44, 54–60, 126 n. 27, 138
British Council 102
British Museum 37, 38, 126 n. 28
Brooke, Rupert 32, 91
Brookner, Anita 128 n. 29, 135, 138, 139
Browning, Robert 34
Brownjohn, Alan 123 n. 47
Bunyan, John: *Grace Abounding* 44
Burne-Jones, Edward 22–6, 28, 37, 123 n. 7: *Briar Rose* 23, 24; *Green Summer* 22

INDEX

Burne-Jones, Georgiana 22, 24, 25
Butler, Samuel 110
Byatt, A. S. 7, 52, 60, 95, 111, 114, 121 n. 17, 126 n. 34, 129n 15, 135, 139: *Possession* 93
Byron, George Gordon, 6th Baron 34: *Don Juan* 40, 100

Cambridge University 26, 27, 29, 30
Camus, Albert 19
Cary, Joyce 123 n. 47
Carlyle, Thomas 25
Carr, J. L. ('Jim') 13, 122 n. 21: *Month in the Country, A* 100
Carrington, Dora 123 n. 1
Carroll, Lewis 123 n. 1
Cavafy, C. P. 17
Chamot, Mary 78
Chekhov, Anton 77, 79
Cherwell 2, 9, 102, 128 n. 2
Chesterton, G. K. 110
Churchill, Winston 59
Clark, Kenneth 39
Coixet, Isabel: *Bookshop, The* (film) 113
Coleridge, S. T. 21, 99
Colvin, Sidney 25
communism 70
Connolly, Cyril 19
Conquest, Robert 123 n. 47
Cooper, Gary 12
Coppard, A. E. 11, 15
Cory, William Johnson: *Heraclitus* 31
Coward, Noel: *Private Lives* 81
Cripps, Milo 123 n. 47
Cunningham, Valentine 125 n. 19, 139

Dahl, Roald 123 n. 1
Dante, Alighieri 40, 76: *Inferno* 48, 76; *Purgatorio* 76; *Vita Nuova, La* 77
D'Arcy, Ella: 'Irremediable' 35
Davie, Donald 123 n. 47
Day, Thomas 91
Day-Lewis, Cecil 18
Delafield, E. M. 19: *Diary of a Provincial Lady* 112
de la Mare, Walter 16, 19, 32, 86, 108, 123 n. 1: *Peacock Pie* 2
de la Motte, Friedrich, Baron Fouqué 23
de Morgan, William 25
Derrida, Jacques 39, 125 n. 7, 136
Dibdin, Michael 68, 127 n. 4
Dickens, Charles 60, 73: *Dombey and Son* 63; *Pickwick Papers* 16
Digby, Sir Kenelm 23
Dooley, Christina Rose ('Tina') (daughter) 3, 109, 129 n. 14
Dooley, Terence (son-in-law) ix, 107, 128 n. 36
Doyle, Arthur Conan 41
Dostoevsky, Fyodor 79
Duckworth & Co (publishers) 41, 132, 140
du Maurier, George 25
Dunsany, Lord (18th Baron) 19

Eliot, George [Mary Ann Evans] 8, 21
Eliot, T. S. 18, 34: *Four Quartets* 17, 52; 'Journey of the Magi' 109; *Love Song of J. Alfred Prufrock, The* 52, 54–5
Euripides: *Hippolytus* 77
Eurovision Song Contest 112

Farjeon, Herbert 64
Faulks, Sebastian 114
Ffrangcon-Davies, Gwen 10
Fichte, Johann 68, 94, 100
Fitzgerald, Christina Rose

144

INDEX

('Tina') (daughter), see Dooley, Christina Rose ('Tina')

Fitzgerald, Desmond John Lyon (husband) 3, 9, 37, 42, 48, 52, 53, 69, 86, 109, 112, 136: *History of the Irish Guards, A* 129 n. 5; 'Soldier in My Throat, The' 102, 129 n. 5

Fitzgerald, Edmund Valpy (son) 3

Fitzgerald, Maria ('Ria') (daughter) 3, 4, 38, 112

FITZGERALD, PENELOPE MARY allusions, quotations, echoes, uses of 7, 11–12, 17, 22, 29, 37, 40–1, 44, 50, 52, 62–4, 68, 71, 76-7, 83–4, 86, 91–4, 99, 109–10, 125 n. 23, 134; art, moral purpose of 7, 18–19; body, mind and spirit, interest in 1, 6, 7, 16, 22, 25, 27, 30, 43, 67, 91, 106; details, observation of 7, 11, 13, 22, 101, 104, 112; diction 46, 68, 81, 94; distillation, compression, omission, art of 1, 6, 7, 30–1, 68, 71, 101; downtrodden, the, feeling for 1, 7, 20, 37; emotion, restraint of 8, 9, 10, 16, 20, 25, 27, 30, 38, 45, 53, 86, 112, 116; expectations, subversion of 1, 27, 67, 68, 71, 103, 116; flowers, symbolic language of 24, 94; lyricism, appreciation of 12, 16-17, 40, 97, 108; macabre coupled with the ordinary, taste for 6, 14, 90, 101; narration, style of 7, 10–11, 14, 20, 28, 34–5, 40, 51–2, 55, 61, 68, 71, 73–5, 90–1, 94, 96–7, 102, 104–6; place and time, evocation of 1, 22, 36, 50, 61, 67, 68, 71, 97; plots, circularity of 14–15, 47; sources, reworking of 6–7, 22, 26, 29–30, 77–8, 80, 81-3, 86, 88, 99, 101; speech (direct, free indirect, reported), uses of 7, 15–16, 28, 30, 37, 57–8, 60, 61; syntax 7, 50, 58, 68, 94, 96; time shifts (prolepsis), uses of 49, 68, 71, 72–3; tragedy treated as comedy 1, 6, 9, 44, 47, 61, 72, 94, 101; wit, uses and opinion of 1, 6, 11, 12, 16, 18–20, 26, 27, 30, 37, 40–1, 47, 53, 63, 100–1, 103, 112, 116, 122 n. 29, 135; writing, reasons for 19

WORKS CITED AND DISCUSSED:
Biographies:
Charlotte Mew and Her Friends 5, 21, 25, 32–5, 67, 117, 120 n. 9, 132, 139, 140, 141, 142
Edward Burne-Jones xiv, 5, 21, 22–6, 27, 28, 38, 110, 128 n. 25, 132, 139
Knox Brothers, The 5, 21, 25, 26–31, 38, 92, 110, 132, 139, 140, 141, 142
Collections:
House of Air, A 1, 2, 5, 7, 8, 9, 15, 16, 19, 56, 60, 88, 100, 101, 103, 116, 133, 141
Means of Escape, The 5, 102–8, 128 n. 1, 130 n. 1, 133, 139, 140, 141
So I Have Thought of You 5, 36, 37, 44, 94, 95, 102, 107, 111–12, 133, 140, 141
'Thirteen Poems by PF' 129 n. 13
Magazine reviews, contributions:
'Arts in Modern Spain, The' 109

145

INDEX

'Feast of the Writers in Tisshara, The' 41, 102
'Letter from Tisshara, A' 41, 102
Novels:
At Freddie's 3, 5, 32, 36, 37, 48, 54, 60–6, 113, 132, 137, 139, 140, 141, 142
Beginning of Spring, The 5, 14, 25, 29, 31, 54, 67, 68, 78–86, 96, 107, 111, 114, 127 n. 13, 132, 133, 139, 141, 142
Blue Flower, The 1, 5, 25, 26, 31, 35, 38, 44, 67, 68, 71, 75, 78, 81, 84, 92, 93–100, 113, 114, 127 n.13, 128 n. 32, 133, 135, 136, 138, 140, 141
Bookshop, The 3, 5, 25, 30, 36, 42–7, 48, 53, 54, 59, 87, 113, 125 n.19, 132, 133, 134, 136, 139
Gate of Angels, The 5, 14, 25, 31, 44, 67, 68, 73, 78, 80, 87–93, 127 n. 13, 132, 133, 135, 137, 139, 140, 141, 142
Golden Child, The 5, 14, 25, 30, 36, 37–42, 74, 79, 103, 132, 136, 139
Human Voices 3, 5, 36, 38, 48, 52, 54–60, 78, 80, 113, 132, 133, 138, 139, 140, 141, 142
Innocence 5, 11, 13, 14, 31, 32, 38, 67, 68, 69–78, 80, 81, 96, 121 n. 13, 127 n.7, 132, 133, 139, 140, 141, 142
Offshore 1, 3, 5, 13, 25, 36, 48–54, 58, 60, 73, 102, 126 n. 31, 130 n.1, 131 n. 12, 132, 133, 137, 140, 141, 142
Poems:
'Arrival of a Stray Cat in the Poet's Lodgings' 129 n. 13
'Autumn: Departure of Daughters' 109, 129 n. 13

'Como El Vilano' (trans.) 109, 118–19, 129 n. 12
'Father and the Mother, The' 109, 129 n. 13
'Feeling and Reason' 109
'G. B. S.' 109, 118
'Invitation from the Poet to Visit His Lodgings at 87a Underdone Road, An' 129 n. 13
'Jug Poem' 129 n. 13
'Kitchen Drawer Poem, The' 109, 110, 129 n. 13
'Late Autumn: The Prophet at the Bus Stop' 110, 129 n. 13
'Later Middle Ages, The' 129 n. 13
'Letter from a Creditor to a Poet' 129 n. 13
'Lover's Humble Request, A' 129 n. 13
'Queue, The' 109, 119, 129 n. 12
'Record Player Poem, The' 129 n. 13
'Veteran, The' 108-9
'White Square Letter Poem, The' 110, 129 n. 13
Short stories:
'At Hiruharama' 105, 107, 111
'Axe, The' 4, 103, 106
'Beehernz' 103
'Curious Incident, A' 128 n. 2
'Curse of a Literary Education, The' 128 n. 2
'Desideratus' 105, 106-7
'Desirable Resident, A' 128 n. 2
'I Was Afraid' 128 n. 2
'Likeness, The' 103
'Look Stranger' 128 n. 2
'Means of Escape, The' 104–5, 106, 108
'Mooi, The' 102, 129 n. 4
'Not Shown' 101

INDEX

'Our Lives Are Only Lent To Us' 104
'Prescription, The' 103
'Red-Haired Girl, The' 103
'Soldier in My Throat, The' 102, 129 n. 5
'Wicked Words' 128 n. 2
'Worlds Apart' 102, 129 n. 6
Unpublished/unfinished/lost works:
biography of L. P. Hartley 21
'Find, The' 103
Iron Bridge, The 42, 103, 125 n. 15
'Matilda, Matilda' 103
Sale or Return 42, 125 n. 15
'Victoria Line, The' 103
'Why (or 'How') We Were Very Young' 124 n. 1

Flaubert, Gustave: *Madame Bovary* 100
Fletcher, H. Lynton 55
Flint, F. S. 111
Flower, Dean 7, 102, 121 n. 15, 125 n. 11, 128–9 n. 2, 130 n. 10, 135–6, 139–40
Forster, E. M. 1, 11, 35, 116, 120 n. 1, 121 n. 7: *Howards End* 35
Fraser, Eugenie 81
Fraser, Ronald 16
Freeston, Miss 61
Frost, Robert 34

Galvin, Patrick 123 n. 47
Gardam, Jane 115, 140
Garnett, Constance 79
Gaskell, Elizabeth: *Cranford* 59
Gaskell, May 23
Germany 28, 67, 81, 93–100, 112
Gibbons, Stella 13
Gibson, Wilfred 34
Gielgud, John 10
Giorgione (Giorgio Barbarelli da Castelfranco) 22
Gissing, George: *The Nether World* 92
Gittings, Robert 123 n. 47
Gladstone, William Ewart 25
Goethe, Johann Wolfgang von 68, 81, 97
Goodman, Elizabeth 33
Gordon, Adam Lindsay 77
Gordon, Edmund 47, 121 n. 1, 125 n. 20, 129 n. 10, 136
Graham, Frances 23
Graham, Stephen 82
Graham, W. S. 123 n. 47
Gramsci, Antonio 68, 70, 74
Grant, Joy 34, 124 n. 17
Gracq, Julien 123 n. 47
Greene, Graham 8
Grenfell, Joyce 19
Grossmith, George and Wheedon: *Diary of a Nobody* 59, 92, 102, 112
Gumbrecht, Hans Ulrich 52, 126 n. 24

Hall, Radclyffe ('John') 123 n. 1
Hamburger, Michael 123 n. 47
Hamilton, Iain 123 n. 47
Hardenberg family 26, 31, 93–100
Hardenberg, Georg Friedrich von, see Novalis
Hardy, Thomas 32, 117, 123 n. 46: *The Mayor of Casterbridge* 99
Harland, Henry 33
Hartley, L. P. 21, 123 n. 47
Harvey, W. J. 4
Harry Ransom Center, Austin, Texas ix, 7, 121 n. 14, 125, 127–8, 134
Haycraft, Colin 37, 41
Headlam, Walter 110
Heine, Heinrich 52, 108, 126 n.

INDEX

31. 'Der Asra' 52, 56
Henchey, Linda 102, 121 n. 2,
  125 n. 11, 129 n. 5, 136
Hennell, Thomas 18
Hensher, Philip 114, 116, 130 n.
  1, 131 n. 16, 136, 140
Hicks, Edward Lee (grandfather)
  2
Hingley, Ronald 81
Hitchcock, Alfred: *Foreign Correspondent* (film) 14
Holden, Inez 123 n. 47
Hollinghurst, Alan 114, 136
Honig, Edwin 21
Hornung, E. W.: *Raffles* 83
Housman, A. E., 32, 108.
  Shropshire Lad 31, 128 n. 42
Huxley, Aldous: *Brave New World* 67

Isis 9, 120 n. 2
Italia Conti Academy 3, 48, 60
Italy 67, 69–78, 114

Jacobs, W. W. 92
James, M. R. 89, 90
James, William 92
Jaspers, Karl 19
Jenkins, Elizabeth 13
Jerome, Jerome K. 83
Joyce, James 19
Jünger, Ernst 106

Kant, Immanuel 100
Ken, Thomas 91, 128 n. 30
Kermode, Frank 4, 31, 53–4, 73, 89–90, 126 n. 25, 127–8 n. 22, 129 n. 9, 133, 140
Keyes, Sidney 18
King, Francis 31, 123 n. 3, 127 n. 7, 140
Kingsley, Charles: *Water Babies* 91

Kingsmill, Hugh 19, 123 n. 46
Kipling, Rudyard 26, 110: *Kim* 26; 'Wireless' 35
Klee, Paul 109
Knight, Christopher J. 130–1 n. 10, 134, 136–7
Knight, G. Wilson 39–40
Knox, Christina Frances (mother) 1–2
Knox, Alfred Dillwyn ('Dilly') (uncle) 2, 26–31, 92, 123–4 n. 9
Knox, Edmund Arbuthnott (grandfather) 2, 25, 26, 124 n. 11
Knox, Edmund George Valpy ('E. V.', 'Eddie', 'Evoe') (father) 1, 2, 26–31, 32, 108–9, 112, 116, 126 n. 30
Knox, Ethel (aunt) 123 n. 8
Knox, Ethel Mary (née Newton) (step-grandmother) 29–30, 31, 116, 124 n. 10
Knox, Oliver (cousin) 69
Knox, Ronald Arbuthnott ('Ronnie') (uncle) 2, 26–31, 41, 112, 124 n. 11
Knox, Wilfred (uncle) 2, 26–31, 54
Knox, Winifred Frances (aunt), see Peck, Winifred
Kock, Ludwig 126 n. 27
Kühn, Sophie von 68, 75, 93–100

Lawrence, D. H. 128 n. 31: *The Fox* 93
Lazarus, Emma 83
Lear, Edward 123 n. 1
Lee, Hermione 131 n. 12, 133, 137, 141: *Penelope Fitzgerald: A Life* ix, 2, 4, 5, 23, 27, 38, 42, 48, 49, 52, 53, 55, 69, 70, 72, 77, 78, 79, 83, 84, 92, 96, 98, 100, 102, 103, 106, 109, 113,

114, 116, 117, 120 n. 8, 123 n. 8, 124 n. 1, 125 n.19, 126 n. 27, 128 n. 32, 129 n. 11, 134, 136, 138
Legros, Alphonse 25
Lehmann, John 21, 123 n. 47
Leigh-Fermor, Patrick 19
Lesser, Wendy 120 n. 9, 127 n. 3, 137
Lévi-Strauss, Claude 39, 124 n. 7
Lewis, C. S. 123 n. 1
Liddell, Alvar 126 n. 27
Lilliput 102, 129 n. 5
Lu, Lian 127 n. 13, 130 n. 10, 131 n. 12, 134
Luckes, Eva 92

Macaulay, Rose 8
MacDonald, George 5, 25, 127 n. 23: *Phantastes* 84, 95
MacDonald family 24, 25–6
Macmillan, Harold 123 n. 47
MacMurray, Fred 13
MacNeice, Louis 16, 17, 18, 19, 123 n. 1
Madox Ford, Ford: *The Good Soldier* 77
Mailer, Norman 19
Malamud, Bernard 19
Malory, Sir Thomas: *Le Morte d'Arthur* 22, 23
Malraux, André 19
Marlowe, Christopher: *Doctor Faustus* 91
Marvell, Andrew: 'The Garden' 97
Masefield, John 32
Maude, Aylmer 82
McBain, John 126 n. 27
McGahern, John 93
McWilliam, Candia 99, 130 n. 6
Melville, Herman: 'Bartleby: The Scrivener' 103; *Billy Budd* 18

Merriman, J. X. 12
Mew, Anna Maria 33
Mew, Anne (Caroline Anne Frances) 32
Mew, Charlotte Mary 32–5, 110, 117, 120 n. 9, 124 n. 15
Miller, Betty 13
Miller, Henry 19
Milne, A. A. 19
Milton, John: *Paradise Lost* 10
Monro, Alida 32, 33, 34, 124 n. 16
Monro, Harold 32, 124 n. 17
Moore, Brian 93
Moore, George 123 n. 1
Moravia, Alberto, 11, 19, 69: *The Conformist* 10
Moravian Brotherhood 25–6, 96, 99
Morris, William 5, 18–19, 22–6, 28, 106: *News from Nowhere* 39
Murdoch, Iris 115, 138
Murrow, Ed 126 n. 27

Nabokov, Vladimir: *Lolita* 43, 47
Neame, Phyllis 42, 43–4, 125 n. 17
Newman, John Henry 25
Nietzsche, Friedrich 39
Novalis 25, 35, 75, 93–100, 111, 127–8 n. 22, 138: *Blüthenstaub* 97; *Fragmente und Studien, 1799–1800* 99; *Heinrich von Ofterdingen* 84, 93

O'Brian, Patrick 113
Oliphant, Margaret 21
Ollard, Richard 61, 114, 124 n. 13, 126 n. 29, 127 n. 9, 130 n. 8, 137
Orwell, George: *Nineteen Eighty-Four* 67
Ostrovsky, Alexander 79
Owen, Wilfred 34

INDEX

Oxford University 4, 5, 9, 19, 26, 27, 28, 102, 124 n. 1, 126 n. 27: Somerville College 2, 120 n. 2

Paderewski, Ignace 23
Pain, Barry 92
Parker, Dorothy 110
Pasternak, Boris 79
Pater, Walter 2
Pavese, Cesare 6, 76
Peck, Winifred Frances (aunt) 2, 4, 29, 30, 123 n. 8
PEN International 69, 102
Petroni, Guglielmo 69
Pitcher, Harvey 81–3, 123 n. 5, 127 n. 12, 131 n. 11
Platonov, Andrei: 'The Return' 79
Poe, Edgar Allan 106
Poetry Bookshop, Bloomsbury 2, 32, 33–4
Pope, Alexander 12
Porter, Cole 110
Powell, Anthony 113
Pre-Raphaelite Brotherhood 24
Presley, Elvis 52
Priestley, J. B. 61
Primrose, Harry, 6th Earl of Rosebery 42
Prinsep, Valentine 25
Pritchett, V. S. 19, 104–5, 129 n. 8
Proffitt, Stuart 111
Prokosch, Frederic 16
Proust, Marcel 40
Punch 1–3, 5, 8, 9–20, 21, 26, 32, 34, 39, 79, 102–3, 108–9, 112, 120–3, 125–7, 133, 141
Pym, Barbara 5–6, 45, 115, 131 n. 12

Queen's Gate School, Kensington 3, 48

Read, Herbert 123 n. 47
Redgrave, Michael 61
Reed, Carol: *Night Train to Munich* (film) 13
Renoir, Jean: *La Règle du Jeu* (film) 92
Rhys, Jean 123 n. 1
Richard, Cliff 52
Richler, Mordechai 93
Rilke, Rainer Maria 18
Robinson, Marilynne 128 n. 33
Rodin, Auguste 10
Rosebery, Lord, see Primrose, Harry
Rossetti, Christina 123 n. 1
Rossetti, Dante Gabriel 23, 24, 76, 110
Rosso, Medardo 10–11
Rowan-Robinson, Christopher 125 n. 17
Ruskin, John 5, 23, 24–5, 28: 'The Queen of the Air' 123 n. 6; *Unto This Last* 44
Russell, Bertrand 19
Russia 1, 38, 67, 78–86, 127, 139, 141
Rutherford, Ernest 68

Sackville-West, Eddie 126 n. 27
St Philip's Cathedral, Birmingham 22, 31
Salinger, J. D. 19
Salisbury, Lord (3rd Marquess) 23
Salzillo, Francisco 14
Sannazaro, Jacopo 76
Sansom, Ian 131 n. 15, 138
Saroyan, William 123 n. 47
Sassoon, Siegfried 32
Sayers, Dorothy L. 123 n. 1
Schiller, Friedrich von 68
Shakespeare, William 6: *King John* 64; *Macbeth* 10; *The Tempest* 63

INDEX

Shaw, George Bernard 109
Shepard, E. H. 19
Shirley, James 109
Shreiner, Olive 12
Simenon, George 13
Sinclair, May 116
Siquerios, David 7
Sitwell, Edith 18, 122 n. 41
Sitwell, Osbert 19
Smith, Stevie 19, 109, 111
Soldati, Mario 69
Sole Bay Bookshop 3, 42
Solzhenitsyn, Aleksandr 79
Spain 14, 18, 86, 112
Spark, Muriel 19, 115, 138
Spender, Stephen 17, 18
Stead, C. K. xiv, 127 n. 7
Steiner, George 4, 120 n. 7
Stephen, Leslie 25
Stevens, Wallace 40, 125 n. 10
Stolypin, Piotr 81
Stonier, G. W. 11, 121 n. 10
Stoppard, Tom 6, 120 n. 9, 138
Strachey, Lytton 115–16
Struther, Jan 19
Sudrann, Jean 138
Sullivan, Arthur 91
Swinburne, Algernon Charles 110

Tallis, Thomas 91, 128 n. 30
Tamiroff, Akim 12
Taylor, Elizabeth 10, 13
Thomas, Dylan 19
Thompson, Abraham 24
Thwaite, Anthony 123 n. 47
Tolstoy, Lev, Count 18–19, 68, 79, 81, 82: *Ivan Ilych* 79; *Resurrection* 79, 83
Tolstoya, Tatyana 79
Trilling, Lionel 11

Tripitaka, 40
Turgenev, Ivan 6, 81: *Fathers and Sons* 77, 79

Underhill, Evelyn 120 n. 9

Vaughan, Henry 117
Virgil: *The Aeneid* 29

Walpole, Horace 106
Waugh, Evelyn 29, 123 n. 1, 124 n. 10, 138
Wells, H. G. 35
West, Rebecca 123 n. 1
Westminster Tutors 3, 36, 48, 61
Whistler, James Abbott 13
Wickham, Anna 111
Wilde, Oscar 23, 122 n. 29
Willans, Geoffrey 19
Williams, Charles, 40
Wilson, Angus, 6, 123 n. 1
Wilson, A. N. 37, 124 n. 2, 130 n. 6, 138
Wodehouse, P. G. 19
Wolfe, Peter 124 n. 2, 130 n. 10, 134
Wood, James 100, 120 n. 8, 125 n. 21, 128 n. 41, 138
Woolf, Virginia 19, 21, 32, 113, 115: *To the Lighthouse* 73
Woolmer, Howard 111
World Review 3, 5, 9–20, 34, 41, 69, 86, 102, 109, 121–5, 128, 129, 131

Yeats, Jack 11
Yeats, W. B. 18, 34
Yonge, Charlotte 23

Zambaco, Maria 23, 123 n. 7